Prejudice to Pride

MOVING FROM HOMOPHOBIA TO ACCEPTANCE

ANN MARIE PETROCELLI

NASW PRESS
National Association of Social Workers
Washington, DC

Jeane W. Anastas, PhD, LMSW, President
Elizabeth J. Clark, PhD, ACSW, MPH, Executive Director

Cheryl Y. Bradley, *Publisher*
Sarah Lowman, *Project Manager*
Sara Jones, *Copyeditor*
Juanita Doswell, *Proofreader*
Karen Schmitt, *Indexer*

Cover by Naylor Design
Interior design by Electronic Quill
Printed and bound by Sheridan Books, Inc.

First impression: January 2012

Library of Congress Cataloging-in-Publication Data

Petrocelli, Ann Marie.
    Prejudice to pride : moving from homophobia to acceptance / Ann Marie Petrocelli.
        p. cm.
    Includes index.
    ISBN 978-0-87101-428-3
    1. Heterosexism—United States. 2. Heterosexual parents—United States. 3. Gays—United States. 4. Lesbians—United States. 5. Families—United States. I. Title.
    HQ76.3.U5P428 2012
    306.76'6—dc23

                                                    2011042726

Printed in the United States of America

Table of Contents

Acknowledgments

During the years that I worked as a singer/songwriter/musician, I had the pleasure of working with many phenomenal professionals in the music industry. One such fine artist was Otis Blackwell, a renowned songwriter who composed "Don't Be Cruel," "All Shook Up," and "Return to Sender" (with Winfield Scott) for Elvis Presley. He also received credit for composing "Great Balls of Fire" and "Breathless" for Jerry Lee Lewis and "Handy Man" for Jimmy Jones. In the time Otis and I worked together, he taught me the key ingredients to song composition. Otis was a quiet man of few words. When he talked, everyone listened because his words were powerfully educational. One day, I remember Otis telling me that when you know the title of the song, then you know the whole song. At first, I did not understand the words. As I continued to write songs, however, it became clear to me what Otis meant.

I geared the writing of *Prejudice to Pride* around the "hook line" title. A *hook line* in a song is defined as catchy words that are easily remembered and recur throughout the song. With *Prejudice to Pride* as the book title that came to me, I immediately recognized that it fulfilled all the requirements of a hook line and would serve as the guide to writing the book. Although writing songs is a different art form than writing books, I learned from working in both milieus that all art forms are one art form, and that which is used in one art form is applicable for use in another.

Part of my history includes 10 years as a New York City (NYC) yellow checker cab driver. This type of work helped me to learn the geography of the greatest city in the world and meet people from all walks of life. I learned about the different personalities of people and their needs, wants, goals, passions, loves, problems, prejudices, and sufferings. The knowledge and experience I gained from being a cab driver came in handy while earning an MSW degree at New York University. It is really true what they say about cab drivers being like therapists. I would even venture to say that the unique combination of driving a cab and being a licensed psychotherapist helped me to develop keen and outstanding clinical skills that have helped many.

From the age of 15 and on through adulthood, I received a salary working in nursing homes, hospitals, hospices, and outpatient clinics. To date, I have obtained the titles of skilled medical social worker, psychotherapist, and director of a program working with adults with mental illness. In retrospect, I find that it is rare to possess the type of resume I do. Driving a taxicab in NYC helped me become street smart. Being a singer/songwriter/musician developed the artist in me. Completing graduate school cultivated my academic side. Working in hospitals, nursing homes, hospices, and outpatient clinics helped me to understand that everyone suffers, that life is short, and that a life lived with empathy is a life lived with bliss. To all those people whose paths I have crossed while working, I thank you for helping me to become the person I am and for the experiences that helped shape this book. You will always be remembered and hold a deep and loving place in my heart.

Thank you, NASW Press Publisher Cheryl Bradley, Lisa O'Hearn, Sara Jones, Sarah Lowman, Sharon Fletcher, the book committee, and all other contributors for your brilliant work, generous spirit, and kindness. Last but not least, I thank Terry Ann for being the friend, soul mate, and treasured gift that life bestowed upon me. Without you, *Prejudice to Pride* would still be an idea waiting to be written. With you, the pages hold more meaning and the meaning of my life takes on a whole new sparkle. May God and our love continue to guide us to help others as we continue to grow ourselves. Always remember, Terry Ann, I love you.

About the Author

Ann Marie Petrocelli, LMSW, is a Brooklyn, New York, born-lesbian and an MSW graduate from New York University. She is the program director of a 168-bed supportive housing residence for adults with severe and persistent mental illness. Recently, Ms. Petrocelli moderated a workshop titled "The Unique Challenges and Benefits of Serving LGBTQ Tenants in Supportive Housing" as part of the 11th Annual New York State Supportive Housing Conference held in New York City. She has also facilitated numerous groups consisting of transsexual members at the LGBT Center located in Greenwich Village, New York.

Introduction

Prejudice to Pride captures past to present attitudes about gay men and lesbians from the point of view of the heterosexual majority as well as from individual out and closeted gay men and lesbians. It describes a sojourn moving away from ignorance and false beliefs about gay men and lesbians toward increased understanding and support of the gay community. The prejudice-to-pride path specifically names the supporters of the gay and lesbian movement; explains what enables the gay movement to travel positively and consistently forward; defines and describes the fuel that sustains healthy movement; points out who and what deters from positive gay travel and how; and discusses the ways to remove and prevent barriers from impeding the progress of the gay movement.

While I was writing the book, thoughts arose that I had never before realized. I believe that constantly confronting discrimination from new angles decreases hate and increases support of the gay and lesbian community. The novel ideas contained in *Prejudice to Pride* do just that. They help reeducate heterosexist people and provide the momentum needed to continue to propel the gay movement forward.

The more people get together to develop and promote unique and varied perspectives on how to increase gay protection and decrease homophobia, the sooner gay men and lesbians will gain all of the rights that straight people have enjoyed for centuries. If the book helps others as it helped me, then it will have served its purpose by giving society the gift of increased knowledge about gay people and the attitude that gay people are beautiful people.

The reasons for writing *Prejudice to Pride* are threefold: personal, educational, and political. Personally, the knowledge and experience contained in this book represent 56 years of living as a lesbian in New York. The actual writing of this work helped crystallize my life to move to the future with a different perspective than if had I not written it. It enabled me to see my own past and present levels of internalized heterosexism and homophobia, which influenced me to find ways to continuously combat them and, in turn, increase my health and freedom.

What I hope more people will someday realize is that we are all equal and that we all must fight against the barriers that hold us back from equality. Looking back in history, gay people were revered, protected from harm, and valued. They shared in the equal rights of all. Patriarchal society then took away gay people's equal rights, leaving gay men and lesbians in the unwanted position of battling a long history of oppression, discrimination, and prejudice. Personally, this book is my way of helping to regain gay rights through educating more people about the gay community. I hope to help society learn what gay men and lesbians really think and feel rather than to continue blindly believing the myths surrounding the microculture.

The second reason for writing *Prejudice to Pride* is to educate heterosexist people and gay advocates on the truth and myths about gay people to help gain the Constitutional rights of gay men and lesbians. The book serves to unify and raise the consciousness of all people by supporting gay rights as basic human rights. The truth of the matter is that Americans will only begin to experience true equality the day that gay men and lesbians gain full protection and equality under the law.

Persistent discrimination against gay men and lesbians should signal a deep-seated problem in the core of everyone's soul. It should serve as a wake-up call that civility will only advance when discrimination is erased. Until that time, America remains crippled by its ignorance and fear of the gay population. It cannot escape the fact that those who discriminate against others represent a projection on their part that lacks not only respect for others, but also self-respect.

This book contains the knowledge and experiences of gay men and lesbians meant to help people understand who gay men and women really are and who they are not. It serves to help dismiss the myths and replace them with genuine wisdom about gay people. It is meant to help everyone increase their love, civility, and advocacy for gay people, and for all people, so that more people will want to befriend gay people.

I am aware that there will be some who view *Prejudice to Pride* as blasphemous. To these people, I say that I am very grateful that you picked up this book to read. It reflects the beginning of your openness in gaining valid and reliable knowledge about gay men and lesbians. Hopefully, you will begin to realize that heterosexist and homophobic attitudes and feelings help fuel increased statistics of gay hate crimes. Until people genuinely possess the type of mentality and conscience that supports equality for gay people, societies everywhere need to be concerned about their safety and well-being because hatred and fear toward others often represent hatred and fear in oneself. Any society of people that denies equal rights and protection to the gay population will not progress as a civilized society until this problem is acknowledged and expunged.

The third reason for writing *Prejudice to Pride* is a political one. My lesbian life turned into a political lesbian life the day I realized that politics are partly responsible for my lack of equal rights and protection under the law. Politics are guilty of blurring the line between the separation of church and state by allowing laws to be guided by religious groups who hope to deny gay people's rights. The true blasphemy lies in certain not-for-profit religious groups professing love for all and then excommunicating gay people on the basis of discrimination. The monies received by religious organizations are tax-free dollars, which are used to politically influence votes that serve to hurt gay people.

The political system is guilty of not recognizing that the U.S. Constitution is being ignored every day that gay rights are denied. It is guilty of blemishing the beauty of America being known as the land of the free. American politics project the image of a country of tolerance and inclusion for all, but in reality it falls short by recognizing only some of its people as free, equal, and protected under the law but not others. Civility pertains to all, not just some human beings. Therefore, civil rights are truly the rights of gay men and lesbians too.

Prejudice to Pride is divided into five sections and 16 chapters. Section I, Heterosexism in the Family of Origin to Healthy Self-Care, contains the first two chapters of the book. Chapter 1, Gay Children, Teenagers, and Adults from Heterosexist Families looks at the clinical aspects of how heterosexist parents negatively affect the lives of gay people as children, teenagers, and adults. It presents the factors involved in diminishing heterosexism as well. Chapter 2, Problems and Strengths of Gay Older Adults describes this population's knowledge, experience, and life stories as being a valuable asset to increasing all people's productivity, knowledge, and civility. The sad truth, however, tells quite a different story of deplorable circumstances experienced by gay older adults, often occurring during what are supposed to be the golden years, as a result of the chronic effects of discrimination and homophobia.

Section II, Unknown to Known Population, contains chapters 3 through 5. Chapter 3, The "Out" and "Closeted" Gay Populations, discusses why and how gay people remain closeted or come out and the advantages and disadvantages of each lifestyle. Chapter 4, Coming Out Is Not a One-Shot Deal, offers the idea that "coming out" is really an ongoing process rather than a single event in the life of gay men or lesbians. It portrays each coming-out experience as a stepping stone to helping gay people transition from being heterosexist, homophobic, and homocentric to being mentally healthier and advocates for gay people and for society at large. This chapter also looks at the cognitive processes involved in choosing whether or not to come out with each potential coming-out experience. Chapter 5, HIV and AIDS, exposes the role that discrimination plays in continuing to label HIV and AIDS as solely a gay disease. Consequently, this stigmatization is listed as one of several dynamics thwarting the advancements toward finding a cure and preventing those with the disease from receiving the proper quality of care and dignity that every ill person deserves.

Section III, Homophobia to Pure Loving, contains chapters 6 through 9. Chapter 6, The Seven Stages of Coming Out, focuses on discrimination and oppression and how they can be viewed and experienced similarly and differently by gay and other minority groups. The chapter also maps out the inspirational path that one woman traveled, cognitively, emotionally, and behaviorally from prejudice to pride. Chapter 7, Prejudice to Pride, discusses the dual meaning of the title of the book—that is, the *individual travel* of gay men and lesbians from mental illness to good mental health and the history of the gay and lesbian *community travel* from prejudice to pride. Chapter 8, Homophobic Religious Leaders and Members, demonstrates the role organized religious leaders can play in preventing equality for gay men and lesbians. It advocates for the increased presence of religious groups that genuinely reflect love and embrace all people. Chapter 9, Church and Conservative Right-Wing Enmeshment, deals with the type of chronic entanglement that has helped sustain gay oppression and prevented gay people from obtaining the legal right to marry, along with the more than 1,400 rights that marriage affords.

Section IV, Past to Present Views, contains chapters 10 through 13. Chapter 10, Heterosexism, Heterocentrism, Homophobia, and the *DSM*, proposes that social and cultural influences played a huge role in causing gay men and lesbians to experience symptoms of mental illness by labeling homosexuality as a mental disorder in the *Diagnostic and Statistical Manual of Mental Disorders* in 1952. Chapter 11, The Model of Change, describes a new form of self-counseling. It offers a step-by-step approach to replacing unhealthy habits, originating from a homophobic upbringing, with newly acquired healthy ways of living. Chapter 12's New Glossary of Terms reflects society's current level of gay understanding and continues to help move the gay community in a positive direction. Chapter 13, Positive and Negative Energy Ripples, defines these two new terms and gives examples of their effects on the cognitions, emotional well-being, and coping skills of those emitting and receiving them.

Section V, Discrimination to Advocacy, contains chapters 14 through 16. Chapter 14, Acknowledging the Harm that Discrimination Causes, serves as a wake-up call for people to realize the long-lasting damage caused by discrimination and homophobia. This chapter lists 21 ways to continue to develop new attitudes, beliefs, behaviors, and understanding that will increase gay advocacy, protection, and equality. Chapter 15, Gay Education 101, discusses the many ways that gay people are denied equality, support, and protection because of the lack of gay education and support. It specifically names those groups that are not educated about the gay and lesbian community and need to be. The chapter also lists several ways to educate people on gay and lesbian issues and why this issue is so important. Chapter 16, Personal Stories of Gay Discrimination, contains stories of gay experiences of discrimination to verify the urgent need for the inclusion of gay men and lesbians in the laws that already protect heterosexuals.

Prejudice to Pride represents one lesbian's voice that would not be held down any longer. After all, silence in such matters only fosters hate, suppression, and discrimination. Speaking out on gay advocacy is something that all openly gay people need to acknowledge and invest in mentally, emotionally, behaviorally, spiritually, and monetarily.

The time has come for all openly gay people to realize the connection between speaking out and gaining rights and remaining silent and losing rights. At the same time, it is important to recognize that once gay people are no longer closeted, they are at a greater risk of being victims of hate crimes. It is my hope that this book will serve as a catalyst for all people to think more about gay rights and how to protect gay men and lesbians. The advancement of gay rights will create new and different ways to cope with discrimination; educate others to see the light about who gay people really are and are not; influence all people to want to get to know and befriend more gay men and lesbians; help decrease prejudice and violence; help closeted gay people to come out and increase the visibility and numbers of the population; help protect gay men and lesbians; and increase everyone's civility, dignity, advocacy, safety, and pride.

HETEROSEXISM IN THE FAMILY OF ORIGIN TO HEALTHY SELF-CARE

CHAPTER 1

Gay Children, Teenagers, and Adults from Heterosexist Families

Sexual identity is as much inborn as race and ethnicity. Gay people are born gay just as heterosexual people are born heterosexual. If heterosexual people think about it, they might understand that they cannot change their sexual status. Heterosexual identity is never considered learned or chosen. Imagine straight people describing their sexual identity as an orientation or a preference. It is unheard of.

Many heterosexuals are unaware of the fact that they have never spent a single moment of their lives choosing to *not be gay*. Yet they believe and promote the myth that gay status is learned and can be unlearned and changed. This is why some heterosexuals fear that extending equal rights to the gay community will turn the entire population gay. This fear arises out of the heterosexist myths that are so pervasive and used to keep discrimination in place. In fact, on November 4, 2008, this particular myth helped voters approve Proposition 8, which overturned the legalization of same-sex marriage in California.

How do the lives of gay people change if they have been ostracized by their family, religious groups, peers, and community? For one, many gay people experience increased rates of depression, isolation, neglect, abuse, and feelings of hopelessness. Second, percentages of suicide ideation and acts and drug and alcohol abuse increase. Third, hate and other crimes against gay people increase and go unpunished because laws protecting gay people do not exist in many states. As a result, the victims feel invisible and are easy targets. Without laws to protect the gay community, it is as if the crime never occurred. Therefore, the crime, criminal, and victim go unrecognized, and the incentive to repeat the crime increases.

Many heterosexuals hold one set of beliefs for the heterosexual population and another opposite set of beliefs for the gay community. For example, many heterosexuals use the terms *sexual preference* and *sexual orientation* to describe gay identity but not heterosexual identity. First, the two terms do not accurately reflect sexual identity. Second, the terms should be stricken from use because they wrongly imply that sexual identity is learned, preferred, and chosen.

After reading the description of symptoms that some gay people have experienced, it is a wonder that people would question the notion that sexual identity is a chosen or preferred lifestyle. Who would choose to be gay knowing that denial of rights, support, and equality are built into each gay person's life cycle? Who would have chosen to be Black years ago, before the civil rights movement, for the very same reasons?

Where do gay people turn when they have been cast out of their families? The gay community has long served as an extended family for all those disowned gay men and lesbians. "Out" and "closeted" gay family members often turn to bars, where meeting other new and potential gay people is easier because they are out and identifiable. Drinking alcohol in gay bars is commonplace because it is a socially accepted thing to do; gay people often feel happy when they are finally surrounded by other out and identifiable gay people; and it is a stress reducer in environs that can trigger high levels of anxiety and homophobia in gay people themselves (due to the effects of ingrained societal heterosexist beliefs).

However, it should not be taken for granted that gay people are automatically comfortable in the company of other gay people. Reeducation in the form of dismissing heterosexist and homophobic myths followed by the incorporation of real and honest gay education must take place with many gay people before they can feel comfortable in the presence of another gay person.

For more than 30 percent of the gay teenage population, social alcohol consumption and drug use increase through time and eventually become problematic by negatively affecting job, social, legal, and psychosocial status. As a result of inadequate support and protection from familial, social, and legal structures, the following is a list of problems that have plagued the gay community: (1) physical abuse, neglect, hatred, discrimination, and harassment experienced in the family of origin, at school, in the workplace, and in public; (2) vandalism, threats, and assaults in the neighborhood; (3) homophobic verbal attacks such as the use of the words *queer, dyke, homo, pervert, queen, lesbo,* and *fag;* (4) being murdered, depression, suicide, rejection, and decreased coping skills; (5) lack of adequate services and resources in health agencies and schools needed to treat mental and medical health and education for students on sexual identity and the gay community; (6) increased high school dropout rates due to unbearable discriminatory environs; and (7) increased homelessness and injuries sustained through hate crimes, the use of weapons, and being disowned by family and friends. Often, heterosexist people wonder why the gay population looks and behaves differently than the majority. They do not, however, connect the dots regarding the role that hatred and discrimination play in fueling these problems.

When a gay person comes out, a common response by family, friends, and coworkers is a denial of homophobic attitudes. Take this example of a 17-year-old gay male who came out to his father. This father believed that he was not prejudiced and knew how to handle the situation. The father responded to the coming-out event by saying, "Son, people don't need to know that you are gay. Why can't you keep it to yourself? I don't walk around advertising my heterosexuality. You only bring on more problems by coming out. Begin showing that you are a man by keeping the information to yourself." After knowing and loving his son for 17 years, the father unknowingly began the process of unraveling the bond he and his son shared. He started to damage his son's and his own well-being by the use of prejudicial words and the notion that being gay is shameful and must be kept hidden. Continued damage resulted from the effects of chronic denial of prejudice from the father and family-of-origin members.

Another example of heterosexist mentality is the "don't ask, don't tell" policy. The ramifications of this policy can be felt by gay people from childhood through the older adult years and have hurt the gay community by maintaining the community's treatment as second-class citizens; keeping the community in the closet—invisible, separate, and unequal; increasing the percentages of previously incurred psychosocial problems that further damage pride and livelihood; and negatively reinforcing the majority's homophobic stereotypes and discriminatory behaviors.

The "don't ask, don't tell" policy is a long-held tradition of discrimination against gay people that is used in more places than just the military. Most parents are not prepared for their own child to be born gay, lesbian, bisexual, or transgender. Most parents are not educated on how to raise a gay child. Rather, parents usually only know what they were taught as children and adults, that is, prejudice and discrimination against gay people.

This false education includes the denial that their child is gay, the parents ceasing to talk with their child when finding out that he or she is gay, talking to the gay child as if he or she is a pariah, trying to convince the child to keep their gayness to themselves, encouraging the gay child to seek clinical help in disavowing their gayness and acquiring heterosexual identity, or even disowning their gay child.

The damage done to a gay child by this verbal and nonverbal communication and acts of discrimination are severe and often require years of therapy to treat. There are also parents who mistakenly believe that they did something wrong to make their child "this way." This idea tends to put the focus on the parent at a time when the gay child needs the attention and support more than ever. Parents cannot make their children gay. However, parents' negative feelings about homosexuality can pave the way for gay children to internalize the disease of heterosexism and homophobia by teaching the growing gay child to be prejudiced against gay people and by discriminating against their child because of his or her gay identity.

Some parents are often filled with conflicted feelings when finding out that their child is gay. They feel grief and guilt over the loss of their "straight" child yet simultaneously feel love for that same child. The grief and guilt were caused by heterosexist and homophobic teachings, which then caused the parents to isolate themselves. As a result, they were left with little or no exposure to gay education, other parents of gay children, and help for their complicated feelings. Consequently, this long-held oppressive view is truly a disease that affects the heterosexual community as much as it does the gay community. Honest and truthful gay education needs to be established and made accessible to all gay parents, parents of gay children, and heterosexist families in order to obliterate the disorder once and for all, as well as its deadly affects on family life.

When, in the above-listed example, the father told his son that he did not walk around advertising his heterosexuality, nothing could be further from the truth. Heterosexual people proclaim their heterosexuality in subtle and obvious ways every day in conversation. When straight people converse about their husband or wife; their engagement, marriage, or divorce; who they are dating; their sexual activities; honeymoon, vacations; relationship problems; health insurance, taxes; or the present they bought for their spouse, they are simultaneously "outing" their heterosexual identity.

Gay men and lesbians know that many heterosexuals do not know that they are relating their sexual identity in their everyday conversations. Heterosexuals are not attacked daily for being heterosexual. Consequently, there is no need for heterosexuals to think about their sexual identity. They

are, for the most part, on automatic pilot wher
on this topic.

There is no reason for heterosexual conscio
sexual identity is considered "the norm" an
daily that is not questioned. Gay people, on t
of impending danger due to gay discrimina
about daily by gay people, which helps increa
identity in ways that straight people do not

To a certain degree, heterosexual and gay
sets, different senses, different sensitivity l
behavioral communications due to the way heterosexist and homophobic
teachings affect homosexuals differently than heterosexuals. Gay people
feel their inner core attacked in response to heterosexist and homophobic
upbringing. Straight people, more often than not, sense that heterosexism
and homophobia are wrong, and not true, but repress this knowledge in
order to continue to think like the mainstream and not make societal waves.

Gay people know when they are being discriminated against and
whether that discrimination is blatant or subtle. There are people too who
unknowingly discriminate against gay people. Discrimination is not always
a conscious decision. Denial is an example of a defense mechanism that
cultivates discrimination and prevents people from consciously realizing
that they are discriminating when in fact they are.

Both heterosexuals and gay people share the acquisition of heterosexist beliefs and homophobia from their family of origin and society. These
learned false attitudes, beliefs, and fears and then cause a certain percentage
of both gay and heterosexual people to avoid gay people. It is much harder,
however, to keep prejudices intact when heterosexist people become friends
with a gay person and, as a result, disprove the stereotypes through that
actual contact.

Prejudice to pride is a journey that tracks heterosexist education acquired
through childhood and the good that can come when people let go of those
old ways of thinking and use the knowledge gained through gay and lesbian
studies to have healthy and positive interactions with people of all sexual
identities. The prejudice-to-pride journey is traveled by heterosexuals and
gay people alike, because the majority of people are raised to be heterosexist
and homophobic. Indeed, the prejudice-to-pride journey involves suffering.

It is not easy to become aware of, acknowledge, and admit that one's past
and present consist of beliefs and actions that are false and hurt others and
self. It is difficult to face the truth that others have suffered due to one's
own prejudicial words and discriminatory behavior. Suffering as a response

ssion is a healthy response and can be the beginning of the
cated person's embrace of gay people. This suffering helps facili-
grief, loss, and bereavement of the prejudicial and discriminatory
oward gay people and fosters the growth of the newly loving, respect-
l, and empathetic self toward gay people.

When I look back to the late 1960s, the time of the famous Stonewall
Riots and fast forward to present day, I see and feel the advances made
toward gay inclusion and equality. I see and experience more people from
all walks of life traveling on the path from prejudice to pride. I see the difference in people's reactions to the words *gay* and *homosexual* in the sense
that people react more positively to the former term and less positively
to the latter term. I see instances of heterosexual family members reject-
ing gay discrimination and educating others to do the same. I see more
positive changes in people's cognitions, feelings, and behaviors toward gay
people. These positive grassroots changes are what eventually help laws to
be enacted that continue to eradicate discrimination, and increase equality
for everyone.

Those traveling the prejudice-to-pride path know what it feels like to
admit to having hurt someone due to their past prejudices. They know
the shame, guilt, and upset it causes within. They know the importance
of locating and stopping the prejudice and discrimination and replacing
the ignorance and fear with loving and respectful thoughts, feelings, and
acts. The prejudice-to-pride journey is a humbling experience. It is an ever-
emerging, eye-opening, and enlightening experience. It is an experience
that lends itself to increased civility, compassion, consciousness, and conscience among all families and people. It is truly a religious, spiritual, and
educational experience, with love as the guide.

CHAPTER 2

Problems and Strengths of Gay Older Adults

The older adult gay and lesbian populations are a brave and resilient people who have survived a lifetime of discrimination. They are the backbone of the gay community with a wealth of knowledge, experience, and life stories that everyone should listen to in order to increase education about gay people. However, the reality is that gay and lesbian older adults are still an invisible population, albeit less so now than when they were children, teenagers, and adults.

Although older adult gay men and lesbians admit that discrimination and homophobia have lessened from when they were children, they will be quick to point out that both still exist. They emphasize that it is not easy to fight discrimination in senior years when the level of physical energy is decreased. Survival is made harder for gay older adults because of the nonexistent laws that would protect their rights and safety. It should be acknowledged that in the midst of these inequalities it takes an enormous amount of energy to continue to formulate life's journey and plans. For example, because society often fails to recognize and validate gay relationships, the death of a partner can be made even more difficult to recover from when the grief, loss, and bereavement are exacerbated by the lack of acknowledgment by society. It is much harder to help a gay person who is grieving cope with a loss when gay and lesbian bereavement groups are almost nonexistent.

Why should the surviving gay partner not have access to social security survivor benefits, or tax-free transfer of survivor IRA contributions, the way surviving heterosexual mates do? When a gay man dies and the inheritance goes to the family of origin that disowned him instead of to his loving partner of 50 years, the discrimination and griever's suffering are evident in the lack of acknowledgment and validation of the gay couple's relationship.

Today's gay and lesbian older adults grew up being labeled mentally ill by psychiatrists; excommunicated by the clergy; dishonorably discharged by the military; slandered by the media; denounced and ousted by their family of origin; and abused by peers, teachers, schoolmates, coworkers, police, and employment agencies. Today's gay and lesbian older adults remember a time when they did not even entertain the thought of marrying. The topic was a closed book and not up for discussion. Fifty years ago, it was believed by the heterosexual and homosexual communities that gay men and lesbians were considered "less than," abnormal, evil, and not entitled to rights and equality.

The idea of marriage being the legal right of gay men and lesbians was not considered years ago because discrimination against gay people was so deeply entrenched in society. The thought of fighting for the legal right of gay men and lesbians to marry through most of the 20th century was an anachronism. It was like a caveman finding a clock in a cave; that is, it was an impossible occurrence whose time had not yet come and could not be told. Years ago, discrimination against gay men and lesbians was believed in without any hesitation. Most people, including gay men and lesbians, did not give the lack of rights and inequality a first or second thought. There was nothing to think about and no actions that could be taken to oppose the inequality. It was automatically understood that the topic of gay men and lesbians was not to be touched, much less fought for.

Gay men and lesbians were to be avoided, abandoned, abused, isolated, and rebuked. Gay and lesbian rights were not supported by heterosexist society. This was at a time when heterosexist society represented a much larger percentage of the majority than it does today. Gay men and lesbians were not even supported by the lesbian, gay, bisexual, transgender, questioning (LGBTQ) community as they are today. In short, there was no incentive to come out in the past, when the climate was predominantly one of hostility toward gay people.

Changing and updating the vocabulary used to define and describe gay men and lesbians in a way that will accurately reflect today's gay and lesbian population will help decrease and eliminate prejudice and discrimination;

increase genuine understanding of the microculture; discover the gaps and omissions existing in laws that prevent protection, freedom, and safety; inspire the enactment of new laws to ensure equality, respect, and support for gay men and lesbians; and update the worldview of gay people in a way that accurately matches the population and the current advancements made by gay people and their supporters.

Older adult gay men and lesbians are all too familiar with gay bashing; religious bigotry; degradation; and the hate spewed from the mouths of family, friends, the media, teachers, classmates, police, clergy, and strangers. Older adult gay men and lesbians know what it means to be victims of housing, military, and employment discrimination, police brutality, and medical maltreatment. Older adult gay men and lesbians understand the feeling of loss due to abandonment. They can speak volumes on the experiences of isolation and having no family or children to support their emotional, spiritual, and medical health needs.

Nursing homes and senior-citizen centers consist mainly of heterosexual older adults and a small percentage of closeted gay men and lesbians. A percentage of older adult residents and medical staff are heterosexist and homophobic, leaving no room or incentive for gay and lesbian older adults to come out and find true camaraderie, understanding, services, treatment, and comfort at the end of life. While heterosexuals have paths laid out that guide and help fulfill their lives and needs and passions, gay men and lesbians need to create their own paths to find fulfillment. Otherwise, if gay men and lesbians follow heterosexual paths, they will surely find discomfort, discrimination, and lack of understanding and protection. Heterosexuals travel paths of comfort knowing that their sexual identity is supported, reinforced, and protected. Gay men and lesbians trying to travel the same path as heterosexuals are sure to be denounced and isolated. Therefore, older adult gay men and lesbians forge on with less energy to cope with years of discrimination that just keeps on coming.

Senior housing is built on a foundation of the "don't ask, don't tell" policy. The policy is not blatantly written anywhere to say that older adult gay men and lesbians are not welcome. It need not be. Discrimination against gay older adults runs rampant through many housing complexes without any rules or policies to protect them or prevent the discrimination. Simultaneously, antigay sentiment proliferates everywhere, both privately and publicly and by many, which only increases the oppressive life of gay older adults.

Picture if you will an older adult lesbian relating her life story to her straight, heterosexist, nursing-home-facility roommate. Can you picture what the straight older neighbor's reaction would be if her own history includes being conservative, right wing, Mormon, and antigay? Can you imagine the older adult lesbian's difficulties while conversing with the straight neighbor? Looking at this scenario, it is not hard to understand what helps to reinforce and maintain gay and lesbian depression and isolation.

When will the older adult gay and lesbian population look forward to a time filled with peace, quiet, comfort, safety, and understanding? When will people begin to understand the damage inflicted on gay men and lesbians through prejudice and discrimination? When will homophobic people realize that their hatred toward gay men and lesbians punishes hardworking, upstanding, loving, productive, taxpaying citizens? When will heterosexist people gain insight into the chronic personality disorder of heterosexism, and seek change and treatment? Will there ever come a day when all people can look forward to one population of people rather than a majority that discriminates and a minority that suffers?

Gay and lesbian older adults should be revered for surviving these battles and coping with a lifetime of discrimination. They should be applauded for creating organizations and businesses that advocate for the community. They should be recognized for having picketed, marched, published books, started gay television shows, cared for those dying with AIDS, participated in strikes, increased education in the schools, and fought for and increased equal rights for gay men and lesbians everywhere.

Ageism is a form of discrimination that is especially abominable because of the population it targets. After investing a lifetime in full-time work, raising children, paying taxes, helping friends and family, and donating to charity—in short, being upstanding citizens—even heterosexual older adults sometimes face the pain of being disregarded by family and society. Gay older adults experience this type of discrimination all of their lives simply because they are gay.

Elder abuse and neglect are on the rise. If one thinks about the added discrimination faced by older gay men and lesbians, it is difficult to imagine that these are truly the golden years for gay older adults. In this scenario, there is definitely no rest for the gay older adult weary traveler. There is little relief from the discrimination, heterosexism, homophobia, abuse, neglect, and lack of education. If gay men and lesbians feel invisible in their teenage and adult years, imagine the invisibility experienced in the older adult years.

While coping with the "negative energy ripples" (see chapter 13 for the definition of the term) of a lifetime without equal rights, equal protection, and safety, gay older adults must also contend with the issues of aging, increased medical problems, physical breakdown of the body, and the lack of specialization of services and resources to appropriately serve the community. The level of support for gay and lesbian older adults only decreases, and isolation increases when their partners and friends die.

When gay and lesbian older adults lose their closest friends, the ones who knew their history and understood their troubles, it can be quite challenging to find new confidants. They might have to limit the amount of information they can share about themselves or take on the difficult task of educating others who might have strong heterosexist tendencies. All this, at a time when life should be easier and comfort, care, and support should be present all the more.

SECTION II

UNKNOWN TO KNOWN POPULATION

CHAPTER 3

The "Out" and "Closeted" Gay Populations

Gay people have been on the planet as long as straight people. The gay population, however, is still very much unknown because closeted gay people cannot be counted and because closeted and even openly gay people often remain invisible due to a lack of acknowledgment through the absence of equal rights, discriminatory policies like "don't ask, don't tell," and the Defense of Marriage Act (DOMA), and the proliferation of heterosexism and homophobia. Hence, no one knows, for example, the total number of gay people having high school, undergraduate, or graduate degrees, the true total amount of gay people's salaries; what types of occupations they fill; where gay people like to vacation and live; their religious affiliations; political leanings; interests and hobbies; or even the number of children they have. The United States completes a census of its people, yet we only know about openly gay people, not those who are closeted. Once again, discrimination prevails with an unknown portion of the gay population remaining invisible and uncounted.

Currently, the estimated number of gay people is inaccurate because the gay population is much larger than just the percentage of counted "out" people. This means that the gay population is likely more than 10 percent of the population. It could be more than 15 percent of the population. Indeed, the number could be higher than 20 percent of the population.

23

The point is that no one really knows how many gay people there really are because active discrimination and ignorance ensure that a certain percentage of gay people will remain closeted. For this reason, gay advocates strive, in part, to decrease discrimination to influence closeted gay people to come out. Subsequently, the gay community could reflect with more validity its true population size, gain more insight into the community, and use that knowledge as leverage to further combat discrimination.

The following is a true story: An openly gay man living with his partner in the southern part of the country worked together on building their house. One of the men was a dentist. The other was an architect. The architect discussed ideas about the house with a straight businessman. The businessman was diplomatic and professional during the conversation, but when the gay man departed his entire demeanor changed. The straight businessman turned to one of his coworkers and spoke angrily about the interaction. "I don't care what they do. I just don't want to know about it. I don't go around telling people about my sexual life. Why should I hear about theirs?" he said.

In the story, the businessman's reaction represents a common one reflected by heterosexist people toward the gay community. It exemplifies how heterosexist people focus on and acknowledge only the sexual part of a gay person's life and do not recognize the educational, economic, social, legal, political, familial, emotional, and religious parts. Heterosexist people often keep their prejudices hidden from gay men and lesbians and fail to understand that gay people, in many ways, lead very similar lives to those of straight people. Discrimination helps keep gay people closeted, which helps keep the gay population unknown, which in turn helps sustain discrimination, therefore creating and maintaining the vicious cycle.

When the majority of people discuss gay people, they do not distinguish between openly gay people and closeted gay people. They lump the two together. Closeted gay people, however, are not counted in the gay population statistics. Instead, closeted gay people fall into heterosexual statistics, thereby making both the heterosexual and gay population count inaccurate. The following two lists have been created in order to distinguish between various aspects of closeted and out gay folks. The first list contains behaviors and beliefs of many closeted gay people, while the second list represents the actions and mindsets of many openly gay individuals.

BEHAVIORS AND BELIEFS OF CLOSETED GAY PEOPLE

1. There is a certain percentage of closeted gay people who belong to religious congregations that denounce and excommunicate homosexual

people. Some closeted gay people remain with the religious group, which acts as a cover to help them pass as straight. They are caught in the conundrum of loving the religion in which they were raised, all the while knowing that this same group would condemn them for who they are. Imagine the mental and emotional toll inflicted upon closeted gay people resulting from participating in these types of "don't ask, don't tell" discriminatory religious organizations. In this instance, closeted people contribute to their own demise by supporting organizations and people who are actively antigay and by silently feeling the effects of exposure to two types of heterosexists, those who openly discriminate against gay people and those who believe that their discrimination is hidden when they assume they are in the company of only heterosexuals. By supporting religious organizations that discriminate against gay people, closeted gay people unwittingly support the increased danger felt by openly gay individuals.

2. The closeted gay person often remains that way for reasons of fear and is dishonest with himself or herself and others on a daily basis by not coming out. Lies beget lies, and this only serves to keep the closeted gay person from knowing and acknowledging his or her true self. This kind of life is really not a life. Rather, it is an existence of fear sure to cause depression, distrust, lowered self-esteem, self-abuse, ostracism, isolation, or even suicide.

3. While closeted gay people do not reveal their status to anyone, they are often suspected by the straight population as being different in some way. In this case, because closeted gay people have not overcome their own homophobia and heterosexism, a self-fulfilling prophecy can emerge whereby closeted gay people are often deemed "less than" by themselves and by society. Although it is true that some closeted gay people do not suffer the same blatant discrimination that openly gay people face, it can be said that closeted gay people still run the risk of increased self-damage by being exposed to discrimination.

4. Many closeted gay individuals use this status as a coping mechanism until they are ready to come out. Gay people are not ready to come out until they are ready to come out. Should a person come out before they are truly ready, the consequences could be dire. Closeted gay individuals need to prepare mentally and emotionally, be it consciously or unconsciously, in order to face the subsequent difficulties of coming out. Closeted gay people usually know when they are ready to come out once they reach a certain level of discomfort with personal experiences of heterosexism and homophobia. At this time, closeted gay people should devise a "coming-out" plan to better cope with the impending experience.

5. The Model of Change, a form of self-counseling, is included in chapter 11 to facilitate closeted gay people with the coming-out process. Otherwise, if closeted gay people do not come out, more often than not, they can expect increased suffering in various aspects of their lives. These problems include the validation of heterosexist beliefs about gay people by remaining silent when hearing them.

6. Closeted gay people are more prone to socialize in straight circles for fear of being labeled gay if found in the company of gay people. For this reason, closeted gay people hinder the advancement of gay pride, safety, equality, and freedom.

7. Closeted gay people, while coexisting with only straight and not openly gay people, are in reality, segregated from society, from out gay people, and from each other because they do not belong to a mutually supportive community. They have only isolation to look forward to unless they can banish their own homophobia and reveal their closeted status to someone.

ACTIONS AND MINDSETS OF OUT GAY PEOPLE

1. Out gay people often lead healthier, more positive, honest, and genuinely proud lives than closeted gay people. Openly gay individuals choose to face the prejudices that were initially believed and accepted when closeted. They can work through the prejudices and slowly but surely disprove the false beliefs taught by heterosexist society. Although openly gay people are more susceptible to blatant discrimination than closeted gay people, they also have the advantage of helping themselves and the entire gay community oppose gay abuse and reeducate heterosexist society about the gay community.

2. Out gay people are in the position to eventually erase any and all self-hatred caused by having been closeted. Out gay people serve as role models for and help reeducate closeted gay people and the majority. It is much more difficult for openly gay people to belong to religious organizations that condemn homosexuality because they have already eradicated the need to maintain a false character and will not allow themselves to be hurt by self-deprecation. As a result of being reeducated and gay enlightened, openly gay individuals are more apt to reject religious groups that demoralize them and instead join the kind of religious groups that embrace them and the gay community.

3. Out gay people represent the gay community and lend to its visibility. Gay visibility is paramount to creating and enacting laws that protect and strengthen the community and its struggle for equality.

4. Many out gay people interact with both the straight and
   tions. Out gay people are in a unique position to help
   what true gay people are like. Openly gay individuals fu
   helping straight people dismiss the horrendous lies and
   with which they were raised about the gay community.

5. Out gay people advance the gay movement. They can
   eted gay people to come out and participate in shifting the population
   from unknown to known. Out gay people increase their own mental and
   physical health and well-being simply by being out.

6. Although it is true that the drawback in being out lies in making oneself
   more susceptible to crimes of hate and violence, it is also true that as
   more closeted gay people come out, rates of hate crimes and violence
   should decrease because gay population size, education, advocacy, rights,
   and safety will increase.

7. A gay person's contributions to society can only be recognized as such
   when that person comes out. Subsequently, the majority of people will
   learn, in a very real way that the gay population consists of more than
   just the few gay stereotypes that people see on television or attending a
   Gay Pride parade. As a result of coming out, gay people can finally be recognized for their contributions as doctors, nurses, lawyers, construction
   workers, accountants, teachers, writers, beauticians, designers, parents,
   clerks, sanitation workers, police, models, secretaries, politicians, social
   workers, and as upstanding, productive people working in virtually every
   occupation. In this way, the gay population will continue to move in the
   direction of being viewed by heterosexist society as healthy, valued, and
   caring rather than perverted, evil, and sick.

The out gay community needs to intensify concentration on identifying
closeted gay people and helping them to come out in order to advance gay
quality of life. Out gay people need to invest their time, energy, and money
in educating closeted gay people so that they can come to understand the
drawbacks of being closeted and the benefits of coming out. They need
to help closeted people understand the role that being closeted plays in
hampering their lives and the vitality of the gay movement. They can serve
as role models to guide closeted gay people on the path from isolation to
openness. Travel on this path will benefit all gay people, both individually
and on the community level.

It is of the utmost importance for the openly gay community to help
their closeted brothers and sisters cross the bridge from prejudice to pride.
In this way, closeted gay people who come out will be able to share in supporting and being supported by the gay population and in reflecting the

true scope of the gay population. Usually, when I brainstorm an idea that is important to gay advancement, soon thereafter, I hear that same idea in the media. For example, approximately one year after I thought of the idea that gay people should take one day a year to strike, and enable all of society to feel their absence and recognize their value, I read online that gay people announced their first "day without gay" strike. A group of gay individuals asked all gay people who worked for companies that did not support the gay community to "call in gay" on December 10, 2008. Similarly, I hope that the out gay population will think of more new and creative ways to encourage closeted gay individuals to come out.

I look forward to the day, and I'm sure it will come, when all gay people are protected under one law and share with the majority in equality. In this way, openly gay people will stop having to look over their shoulder and screen their every word. The social climate and environment will help closeted gay people to come out in larger numbers because there will be increased acceptance, civility, and protection and less fear and shame. The day will come when using the terms "out" and "closeted" will end because discrimination will have been obliterated. Being closeted will exist only in history. The days of gay people being segregated from heterosexuals and each other will end. The days of hesitating to come out for fear of being rejected by family members and friends will end and the days of gay people being embraced by the majority will begin.

If people think that acceptance toward gay people has come a long way, they are right. However, bias and discrimination are still prevalent and if you ask any gay person to relate current stories of bigotry and intolerance, I'm sure their story could fill a book. Ask gay people their perspective on not being able to marry or obtain employee-based health insurance for their partners. Ask gay people what it feels like to be rejected by their families and religious groups because of their sexual identity. Ask gay people to relate personal stories of hate crimes stemming from their gay identity. Ask gay people about the depression, isolation, and lack of support endured as a result of being gay. Ask gay people what it feels like to not be legally allowed to adopt children because they are believed to not make fit parents. Ask gay people what needs to change in order to procure equal rights, protection, and safety.

In my 56 years living in liberal New York, I have never once been asked by heterosexuals any of the questions listed above, that is, questions reflecting a certain amount of genuine interest in and empathy toward gay people by heterosexuals. This is a sad but true statement that echoes the majority's poor level of familiarity with and understanding of the gay microculture.

While it is true that both straight and gay people curren[t] gay rights, society still needs more voices speaking out and to listen. The percentage of people not actively participati[n] cacy is what holds gay people back from obtaining equality. of closeted gay and heterosexual people constituting heter[o] still too large and needs to be decreased and eliminated. M[ ] known about gay people and their lives. Heterosexism and homophobia will not magically disappear. Real work in the form of gay education and sensitivity training needs to be implemented in the home, school, workplace, media, place of worship, and political and legal arenas to bring about real change in beliefs, laws, and behaviors.

CHAPTER 4

Coming Out Is Not a One-Shot Deal

While living as a lesbian for over half a century and traveling the path from prejudice to pride, I have come out numerous times, to various types of people, and under different sets of circumstances. Coming out is not a one-shot deal. Nor do I come out to everyone I meet. Personally, I need a real reason to come out. The level of danger must be assessed and deemed minimal before relating my lesbian identity to others. Stress and level of education of the parties involved are taken into consideration. Each coming-out experience varies according to who I am coming out to, and what role I am filling in that moment, the setting, and society's current levels of advocacy and discrimination. For example, coming out to my parents 38 years ago was far more stressful than coming out today to a class of students in a workshop which I facilitated. It was riskier coming out to my parents because I had much more to lose by being rejected by members of my family of origin than by a student in the workshop. Coming out in a gay support group is less dangerous than coming out to a group of people known for being homophobic. Coming out years ago was more stressful than coming out today too, because discrimination and prejudice were higher in the past.

Gay people often come out for more reasons than just outing themselves as gay. For example, when I was a graduate social work student attending a New York university, I remembered a professor who came out during class. She responded to a number of students who complained that the syllabus contained too many articles about the gay population. The professor explained that the university needed to educate the students about the LGBTQ population in order to prevent future countertransference from getting in the way of their clinical work. The professor then came out to the students in class. She explained that the only reason she came out was to emphasize that she was one of more than 85 percent of social work professors who agreed to include added LGBTQ material in their syllabi in order to help ensure the quality education of social work students. In turn, this would lead to more effective psychosocial treatment of LGBTQ clients. She explained to the class that there were far too many clinicians still uneducated about the LGBTQ population and lacking clinical skills to treat them. She further explained that if social workers were already gay educated, there would have been no reason for her to come out to the students and no reason for the syllabus to contain a higher percentage of LGBTQ education.

I have come out to people when the circumstances were such that I could choose to abide by the "don't ask, don't tell" policy or not. For example, when heterosexual colleagues talked about their family and love life while in the workplace and then asked me about mine, I came out in order to avoid lying and remaining silent. When in the company of those making prejudicial statements about gay people, I have helped educate the uneducated and verified the source of the educator by coming out as gay identified. I have come out to other gay people to foster gay unity, strength, and advocacy. I have come out to students who have needed education on the gay population and lifestyle. I have come out each time I marched to help increase gay support. I have come out while participating in the gay parade each year. I came out to my mother and father as a child and as per the guidance of my conscience and conscious mind.

Coming out is the type of experience that will continue throughout the gay person's life. I choose who, when, how, where, and why I come out every single day. Each decision made to come out, or to not come out, is a conscious one. My history of coming-out experiences, how I coped with and responded to them, and each act of discrimination perpetrated against me help to continuously define who I am. This history represents part of what differentiates out and closeted gay people.

Closeted and out gay people differ in that closeted gay people develop a history of experiences where they consciously choose to remain silent rather than come out with each opportunity that arises. They develop a history of how to cope with personal experiences of discrimination by consciously or unconsciously choosing to not come out. This history forms threads of emotion and cognition that affect the closeted person's development in ways that are often unhealthy. With each act of silence, levels of confusion, guilt, depression, stress, isolation, suicidal ideation and acts, and drug and alcohol abuse often increase, while self-esteem, support, and the ability to cope with and understand oneself decrease.

One would think that closeted gay people would want to come out after considering the list of problems that could affect them if they choose to remain in the closet. The daily choice to remain closeted rather than come out is likely linked to that person's heterosexist, homophobic upbringing. The level of heterosexism and homophobia attached to each person's history varies in intensity. Some are raised in less heterosexist and homophobic environs. Some are raised in areas of the country and by families that are highly homophobic and heterosexist. Personal reactions to different levels of homophobic and heterosexist education vary as well. Some gay people reared by highly heterosexist and homophobic families come out, while some remain closeted. The same is true of those raised in homes where family members are less heterosexist and homophobic.

Coming out is an idiosyncratic experience based on many variables, such as a person's essence and personality, make-up of consciousness and conscience, level of education, levels of coping and defense mechanisms, level of exposure to gay individuals, levels of heterosexist and homophobic backgrounds, personal experiences with discrimination, and social climate and conditions.

Out gay people have related that before coming out they often chose to remain closeted due to fear of rejection, ostracism, isolation, and being discriminated against. Experience has shown that these problems are usually felt more intensely when a person is in the closet. The process of coming out can positively affect the way a person copes with depression, hopelessness, lack of support, alcohol and drug problems, suicide ideation and act, guilt, isolation, anxiety, confusion, self-esteem, heterosexism, and homophobia.

Openly gay people are able to develop support systems and genuine relationships that reflect their true identity as a result of coming out. People who are open about their sexual identity speak more openly and with less fear. Closeted gay people tend to have moderate to severe trust issues, making it increasingly difficult to develop genuine support systems and compatibility. Closeted gay people are more likely to suffer with borderline personality problems as a result of the internalization of gay prejudice and discrimination.

Rather than lying on a daily basis about an aspect of your identity, living openly and being one's genuine self is truly a healthier way to live. By responding to and learning to cope with the bias and discrimination in daily life, openly gay individuals achieve the education and improved self-esteem that closeted gay people do not. If it weren't for openly gay people, many more gay people would remain closeted. After all, those who were previously closeted but who now live openly should be considered the most experienced people for helping the closeted to come out. For these reasons too, out gay life is known to be more productive and positive than closeted life.

Closeted gay people who believe that they can pose as straight in society and still educate others about gay people are sadly mistaken. You can only give to others what you already have. You cannot teach what you do not know or understand. Let us compare the effectiveness of out gay versus closeted gay people in teaching others about gay life and discrimination. Who is better able to discuss discrimination, a person who has repeatedly and actively responded to, and coped with acts of personal discrimination or a person who remains silent about his or her gay identity when confronted by personal acts of discrimination? Who is more qualified to educate gay people when they first come out, the closeted gay person with no real experience and knowledge of living openly and honestly, or the person who can put himself or herself in the shoes of the recently out gay person and help to guide, comfort, care for, educate, and support that brave soul? The answer to both questions is the out gay person, for obvious reasons.

Coming out takes a tremendous amount of mental and emotional energy for everyone involved. When you think about how many times a gay person will have to come out in a lifetime, you begin to realize what an enormous task it is. The education and experience gained from each coming-out experience could easily be listed on a résumé aiming for the desk of a CEO interested in hiring a professional gay advocate.

Despite the clear benefits of living openly as a gay person, no one should ever out another person. If a person hears that someone is gay from an outside source only, then this is hearsay and not considered factual or believable. In other words, only if someone personally reports that he or she is gay should an outing be considered factual, accurate, and genuine.

Another way to examine the differences between people living openly or in the closet is to look at a relationship with God, if applicable. Often, closeted and out gay people spend years in contemplation of the validity of God's existence because, according to all of the world's major religions, God is portrayed as unloving toward gay people and because of the ironies of these religious teachings; the persecution imposed on gay people by religious leaders and their followers; how to respond to the hatred emitted toward gay people by religious groups and organizations; and rebirth, which perceives God as all loving, nondiscriminating, and without gender or composed of both male and female gender. However, these considerations influence closeted and out gay people differently, because out gay people are more likely to disengage from discriminating religious groups and their homophobic beliefs, whereas closeted gay people might remain in the prejudicial environment and feel the negative effects from it.

Religious groups that discriminate against gay people might in fact turn that person away from God. What healthy-minded person would belong to a group or praise a God who condemns his or her life and spirit? When the Catholic Church excommunicated me because of my lesbian identity, I was irate over the situation and rejected God. At that time, the only God I knew was the one with which I was raised. As a child, I believed that this religious organization had my best interest at heart. I never could have imagined that this support system would eventually turn out to be the advocate of my demise. I consider it a miracle that I was able to come out, search for, and gain new support systems that eventually helped me pick myself up, dust myself off, and continue to grow. These newly obtained support systems helped raise the self-esteem that my childhood support systems helped raze.

My current relationship with God evolved, in part, because of the influence of heterosexist society. It is a relationship that I discover day by day. It is a relationship that differs greatly from one experienced by closeted gay people who never deviated from the heterosexist religion in which they were born and raised. My initial relationship with God was an inherited one. My newer path and relationship with God is an acquired one, which grew from my dissatisfaction with a religion that would not accept me for who I truly am. These same people who reject me because I am an out lesbian mistakenly believe that God holds these same beliefs. What they fail to realize is that these particular negative beliefs about gay people, which they attribute to God's teachings are, in fact, uneducated and inaccurate interpretations made by religious leaders.

There are as many variations of out and closeted gay people as there are variations of religious beliefs, sexual identities, and races. People should not be demoralized, hated, and killed simply because they are not part of the majority. This type of behavior begets bullying, abuse, crimes of violence, and discrimination, which is not God-like and therefore begs the implementation of education to undo the damage. It is a blessing to be excommunicated from and not be a member of any religious organization that discriminates against people. Many openly gay people are able to work through the grief caused by religious segregation, discrimination, and ostracism and, in so doing, can evolve into genuinely loving, religious, and spirited people.

I ask heterosexuals and closeted gay folks to really consider the pain and challenges of living openly. Consider the pain of being turned away by family, religion, and friends because of sexual identity. Consider being excluded from the laws that protect and provide the majority with equal rights. Consider the trauma of being a victim of a hate crime because of sexual identity. Consider the pain of hearing derogatory slurs and insults day after day. It is not hard to see how these problems can manifest through depression, alcohol and drug use, suicide ideation and acts, homelessness, isolation, and segregation stemming from the continuous bombardment of prejudice and discrimination. While considering the plight of an openly gay person, I ask all heterosexuals to consider: Who would choose to be gay knowing the kind of life one might face? If you think that being gay is a lifestyle preference, then at what point did you choose to be straight?

CHAPTER 5

⚊

HIV and AIDS

Gay men and lesbians cannot legally donate blood or organs simply because of the risk of HIV and AIDS. This is despite the fact that lesbians have the lowest levels of infection with HIV and AIDS of all people, gay or straight. The American Medical Association (AMA) is well aware of these statistics. Although municipalities constantly cry out for blood donations, they still discriminate by not allowing lesbians to donate blood. The ignorance is mind boggling, especially given that all blood is tested before it enters the system.

Since 1985, the Food and Drug Administration (FDA) has had a ban on sexually active gay men donating blood. These policies were enacted when the first cases of HIV and AIDS were being diagnosed and when the medical community still knew very little about the disease. This ban is outdated, and it should be reconsidered. Lesbians should not be automatically banned from donating blood given that the group has such a low risk of infection with HIV/AIDS. Rather, lesbians should be recruited for blood donations because the blood supply of this group is the safest of all people. Yet lesbians are once again targeted by discriminatory policies by being lumped together with gay men simply because of a shared, same-sex sexual identity.

The negative energy ripples that come from bigotry and discrimination have corrupted the minds, hearts, and souls of human beings to believe that gay people's blood is a source of contamination to the country's blood supply. According to many religious groups, God cursed gay men with HIV and AIDS. Why not then say that God blessed all lesbians since lesbians have the lowest percentage of HIV/AIDS status of all people? Is the FDA not confident in the AMA's blood testing? Or do straight people have a problem with gay men's and lesbians' blood entering their system? How deeply engrained is prejudice when a straight person might choose to reject the blood from a gay man or a lesbian rather than save his or her own life?

The uneducated and ignorant perspectives on HIV and AIDS have sent negative energy ripples around the world. There is still too little known about this deadly disease and how it will be cured. When HIV/AIDS first came to the forefront in the 1980s, it was thought to be specific to the gay population. I remember NYC in the early 1980s, when people set up tables at Sheridan Square, in Greenwich Village, to pass out literature on HIV and AIDS. Regardless of their sexual identity, people were in shock over the onset of the disease. Whereas people dying of cancer or heart disease maintained their dignity, and were cared for by family and friends, gay men dying of AIDS did not find the same comfort. They were treated as pariahs and died isolated, depressed, and stripped of their dignity and humanity. HIV and AIDS first gained national attention in the late 1970s and early 1980s. However, I remember from as far back as the 1960s, gay men experiencing the symptoms of what we now know to be HIV/AIDS. Not until the 1990s, when these same men died of AIDS, was the disease finally recognized as having been in existence since as early as the 1960s.

In the early 1980s when HIV was first diagnosed, many people were afraid of the illness because they did not know if it was contagious or how it spread. The disease itself, and those who contracted it, were discriminated against. Even some medical staff behaved in discriminatory ways by not wanting to treat those infected with HIV and AIDS. Gay men suffered shock and complicated grief, loss, and bereavement due to the tremendous amount of friends lost to AIDS and its attack on the community. Many were left immobile, confused, and hurt by the catastrophic number of gay people dying from AIDS and the stigma attached to the disease. During this time, gay and straight women gained strength by supporting and participating in active feminism.

Lesbians and straight women applied their feminist education and experience to help these gay men who were dying from AIDS. Many straight and lesbian feminists learned to advocate for women's rights, monies, and equality. They carried over this knowledge and experience to help mobilize gay men to do the same. Lesbian and straight feminists were the catalysts to help gay men to join in the struggle to increase awareness of HIV and AIDS research to help better understand and find a cure for the disease; the fight against homophobia, and stigmatization of the disease; the provision of direct services to those dying from the illness; the prevention of the disease; safe-sex education; and funding for the cause. These feminists helped create Gay Men's Health Crisis, a nonprofit, predominantly volunteer-run organization that addressed HIV and AIDS issues. Their work truly helped put the disease in the public consciousness and let people suffering with HIV/AIDS know that their issues would be heard and addressed.

With more research and education it was determined that HIV/AIDS wasn't limited to the gay population or IV drug users. It is now known that, in fact, straight men, women, teenagers, children, babies, and newborns are at risk for contracting the disease. Education on HIV/AIDS, and other sexually transmitted diseases (STDs) needs to be increased at home, in the schools, and in the media, particularly because STD rates are on the rise. Regrettably, the topics of sex, sexual identity, and drugs remain taboo in America. Subsequently, education on these issues has suffered. Many teenagers today are woefully misinformed about safe sex as a means of prevention and underestimate the seriousness of the disease despite the recent medical breakthroughs which have allowed people with HIV/AIDS to live longer.

Presently, LGBTQ and straight teenagers are contracting STDs in record numbers due, in part, to the paucity of education delivered to children at home and in school on: (1) sex education; (2) the HIV virus, AIDS, and the thousands of other STDs that can be contracted; and (3) the causes, treatments, and means of prevention for HIV and other STDs. This lack of education has to do with denial about who can contract this disease; the taboo topic of sex preventing discussion from flourishing; and society ignoring this disease, labeling it as only a gay issue.

There is denial about the number of straight men on the *down low,* having sex with gay men while in committed relationships with women. There is denial regarding HIV and AIDS being a disease limited to the gay culture. Straight parents often mistakenly blame the gay population if their straight teenager contracts the disease, instead of acknowledging their failure to educate about disease prevention. Years of experience has shown that the simplistic, "just say no" approach does not work when it comes to drugs, alcohol, and sex. Instead, truthful, in-depth education needs to occur on these topics.

Despite the medical advancements that have prevented many HIV/AIDS-related deaths, increased education is still needed that will continuously "out" the disease as the serious problem it remains. Increased education is needed to continuously out the harsh realities of this disease, including its continued prevalence, how it is contracted, and by whom. Furthermore, increased education is needed to out the specifics of the disease (that is, HIV testing, how it is treated, self-care, and prevention). Over 25 years have passed since the media began covering the HIV and AIDS epidemic. Advancements made by those studying the disease and those caring for people with HIV have helped increase the collective quality of life for so many. Increased efforts toward HIV/AIDS research and education have helped to reduce the numbers of people being infected by the disease, to eliminate the stigma attached to the disease, and to safeguard LGBTQ and straight people and the quality of their care, health, and dignity.

SECTION III

HOMOPHOBIA TO PURE LOVING

CHAPTER 6

The Seven Stages of Coming Out

Gay people are born gay. Those who discriminate are not. Rather, heterosexist people learn and transmit discrimination and prejudice to and from their families, peers, teachers, politicians, religious leaders, coworkers, and the media, and from generation to generation. Is it realistic to say that the baseball, football, soccer, and basketball professions do not contain any gay players? People who believe in this type of myth are prime examples of people deeply entrenched in denial. Professional ball players who abide by the "don't ask, don't tell" policy often do so in order to help themselves and their fans maintain the delusion that there are no homosexuals in professional sports. By doing so, they continue to receive the salary, power, and fame while under the false guise of being considered heterosexual. However, regardless of their wealth, fame, and power, people pay a steep mental, emotional, social, behavioral, and spiritual price by remaining closeted.

Where there is prejudice, discrimination, and oppression, there is segregation. Without a doubt, the gay population is a highly segregated group. Out gay people share a history of being segregated from closeted gay people. Out gay people share a history of being segregated from their families of origin, religious groups, schoolmates, coworkers, employment agencies, the legal system, and the majority. They experience segregation from society as a whole when they cannot freely marry or divorce, when denied employee-based health insurance for their partner, when excluded from rights to protect them, and when they must endure verbal assaults and name calling.

Segregation of any type is deplorable and disgraceful. Gay segregation is different than black segregation in that black segregation is so easily recognized and known by all. At times, gay segregation is less obvious in that it is not discussed and sometimes not even realized by most, including gay people. Nonetheless, it exists and occurs daily. It is a terrible kind of segregation because it is active, destroys lives every day, and can often be an afterthought. Segregation separates and helps prevent unity and strength. Segregation leads to isolation, depression, and lowered self-esteem. It can lead to alcohol and drug problems, economic problems, legal problems, and homelessness. It creates and exacerbates problems with family, education, social status, support, abuse, and suicide. Sadly, these problems are rampant in the gay population.

Why do some gay people choose to remain closeted and not come out? Many people fear the discrimination and segregation awaiting them, should they come out. Consequently, they prefer to remain living under *known* horrendous homophobic conditions rather than venture into the *unknown* world of coming out. Nearly everyone, gay or straight, was raised in a heterosexist, homophobic milieu. The majority of people are taught to be discriminatory toward gay people. This homophobia fosters discrimination, segregation, ignorance, and silence. Unless people learn to dispel the myths of their heterosexist and homophobic upbringing and replace the stereotypes with real education about the gay population, they will continue to remain biased against the gay community. Once people can dispel the myths of their heterosexist and homophobic upbringing and replace that with real education about the gay population, they will be on the path of prejudice to pride. The ultimate goal of traveling along this path is the concept of "gay enlightenment."

Americans are raised to be discriminatory toward marginal groups such as black people, Asians, Mexicans, Hispanics, American Indians, Muslims, gay men and lesbians, bisexuals, transsexuals, women, people with mental illness, children, older adults, indigent people, and many other minority groups. Not all people, however, remain discriminatory toward these groups. Anyone can travel the path from prejudice to pride and relearn the truths about the above-listed microcultures (as opposed to the use of the term "subculture," which suggests a culture that is beneath another culture). Those who travel the path from prejudice to pride are involved in the ongoing process of eliminating prejudices and discrimination toward others by becoming educated on, familiarizing themselves with, and eventually supporting the people they were once taught to oppress.

Gay enlightenment is not achieved overnight. The path from prejudice to pride is a lifelong journey; an active, fluid, and continuous path leading away from prejudice and discrimination and toward gay pride and gay enlightenment. It is a loving path involving suffering, growth, realization, consideration, honesty, and empathy. So, how does one travel the path from prejudice to pride?

Gay pride exists, in part, because heterosexism and homophobia exist. Many people who grew up in heterosexist and homophobic families initially accepted the indoctrination without question. They were raised to fear and avoid the gay population. They were raised to believe that the gay population is perverted and sick. They were taught to focus solely on the sexual aspect of the prejudice and discrimination imposed on gay people to ensure that the heterosexism being taught would be successfully accepted by the majority of society.

The gay population is largely looked upon as sexually deviant rather than sexually variant. Hence, the derogatory terms of "fag," "lesbo," "dyke," "homo," "queer," "sicko," "perv," and "freak" are sadly commonplace and rarely challenged. This type of silence helps sustain prejudice. Consequently, it is no coincidence that some of the crimes perpetrated on the gay community are of a sexually abusive nature.

In this next section, I will define the seven stages of coming out, which describe the sexual-identity development of the majority of gay men and lesbians raised in and by heterosexist families and society. I will apply personal life experiences and various sets of concentric and overlapping circles to illustrate and simplify understanding of the stages.

Gay men and lesbians travel from stage 1 through stage 7 on a path that moves from gay prejudice to gay pride (which is described in chapter 7) and from heterosexist and homophobic to gay educated and enlightened. Reaching the seventh stage of coming out represents the achievement of gay enlightenment, and gay pride is at its highest level. The ages at which gay men and lesbians experience these stages may vary widely, because cognitive, emotional, and behavioral development is situational and idiosyncratic.

The first stage of coming out begins at birth. It comprises gay and lesbian individuals raised, for the most part, in heterosexist homes. Birth also represents the first stage of *separation-individuation,* where the neonate begins the process of separating and operating independently from inside the mother's body. During this stage, gay and lesbian children often identify themselves as such, but remain closeted due to the already effective heterosexist and homophobic teachings. The first stage of coming out is represented by three concentric circles (see Figure 1). The smaller, inner circle represents a small percentage of society; it contains gay and lesbian children totally encapsulated within the larger middle circle. This middle circle represents society as a whole. The largest outer circle contains a small percentage of people, that is, gay and lesbian individuals and gay and lesbian advocates. The gay men, lesbians, and gay advocates composing the largest outer circle associate mainly with each other and not with the majority (those in the middle circle).

The smaller inner circle depicts gay and lesbian children being exposed to and learning heterosexism and homophobia and having little or no

FIGURE 1

The First Stage of Coming Out Represented by Three Concentric Circles

The nucleus is not completely darkened at Stage 1, which symbolizes being born without heterosexism and homophobia.

The smaller inner circle contains gay and lesbian individuals from birth.

The larger middle circle contains the heterosexist majority of society.

Broken lines symbolize free movement to and from circles, and within each circle.

The largest outer circle contains gay and lesbian individuals who mainly associate with each other and not with the majority.

Educated gay and lesbian people and gay advocates occupy all three circles.

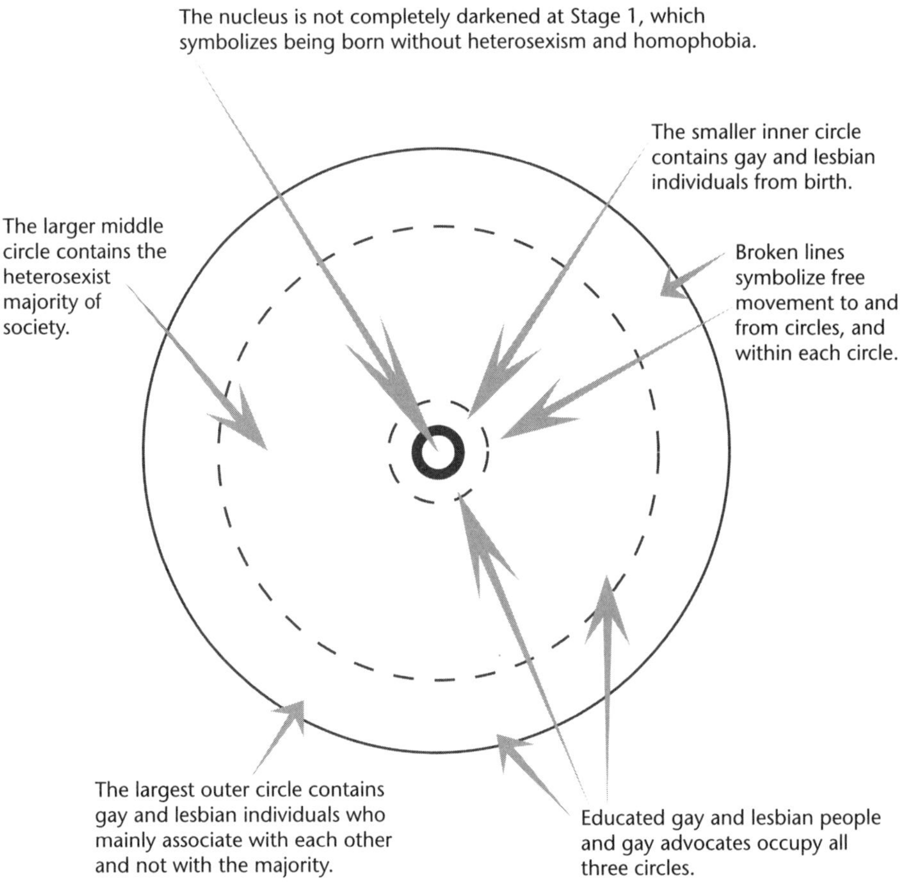

gay contact or gay education. The nucleus is not completely darkened during this time in order to symbolize gay and lesbian individuals born without homophobia and discrimination. The darkened portion of the nucleus represents the overwhelming preponderance of heterosexism and homophobia existing in society and which stands ready to infiltrate the smaller inner circle's nucleus during the person's first phase of separation-individuation. The lines comprising the circumference of the inner and middle circles are depicted as broken lines to depict free movement to and from the three circles.

One lesbian—we'll call her Debbie D—recalled that she realized she was lesbian at age 8 and already knew to keep silent about it because of the negative overt messages and nonverbal messages sent by family, peers, teachers, priests, nuns, friends, and media regarding homosexuals and lesbians. As a result of the negative energy ripples received, Debbie D felt that there was something wrong with her, but she did not know what was wrong, or how, or why. She also remembered times she desperately tried to deny her lesbianism.

In retrospect, Debbie D realized that heterosexism and homophobia were instilled in her long before her adult cognitive maturation developed, which did not give her the option to accept or reject these notions from the beginning. The "don't ask, don't tell" policy invaded her very being long before she could realize that the heterosexist education was false. She was living proof that the prejudices taught by society were effective because they were already internalized by Debbie at age 8.

The crystallization of the assimilation of heterosexism and homophobia by gay and lesbian children from their family of origin and from mainstream society represents the start of the second stage of coming out. During this time, gay and lesbian children still have little or no contact with other gay and lesbian children and have acquired little or no gay education. The three circles representing this stage are the same concentric circles (see Figure 2) depicted in the first stage, with one exception. The nucleus of the smaller inner circle is completely darkened in the second stage to symbolize the assimilation of heterosexism and homophobia by gay and lesbian children.

While in stage 2 of coming out, Debbie D went along with society's agenda and did not challenge or oppose the prejudices and discrimination. She had no knowledge of or contact with openly gay people. She became the self-fulfilling prophecy that heterosexist society intended to create—a closeted lesbian afraid to talk with anyone about her sexual identity.

By the start of adolescence, Debbie D began isolating herself from others after repeatedly listening to children, teenagers, and adults vocalize prejudices about gay people. She became depressed, with lowered self-esteem.

FIGURE 2

The Second Stage of Coming Out Represented by Three Concentric Circles

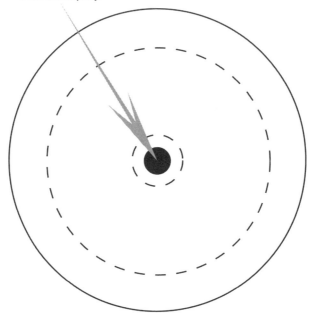

Here the nucleus is completely dark, to represent childhood assimilation of heterosexism and homophobia from the majority.

She remained closeted. The middle part of adolescence represented the beginning of the second separation-individuation phase for Debbie. It represented the third separation-individuation phase for her parents, who were simultaneously experiencing their daughter leaving home and the start of a new and different life beginning for them. The prerequisites needed for an adolescent to leave the nest of the family of origin and achieve healthy independence are confidence, happiness, high self-esteem, and healthy support systems. Sadly, this is not the description of many gay and lesbian teenagers.

During adolescence, Debbie D was fortunate to have met a few individuals who were gay and some heterosexuals who were pro-gay. Consequently, she began to feel dissatisfied accepting heterosexism and homophobia without question while still remaining heterosexist and homophobic. This initial stage of interaction with gay people, and with gay advocates, represents the start of the third stage of coming out and can occur at any age. Here, the concentric circles are repositioned (see Figure 3). The smaller inner circle

FIGURE 3

The Third Stage of Coming Out Represented by Three Concentric Circles

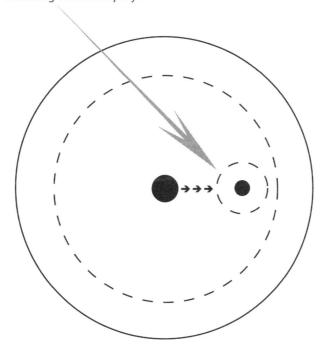

The smaller inner circle (gay and lesbian people) develops its own nucleus. It depicts increased gay education and decreased heterosexism while interacting with the majority.

and the middle circle no longer share the same nucleus. Instead, the smaller inner circle develops its own nucleus and begins moving through the larger middle circle to depict gay and lesbian individuals who are beginning to break free of heterosexism and homophobia and gaining awareness of gay advocacy, gay education, and gay contacts. The first three stages designate the period of time before a person comes out.

It was not until late adolescence that Debbie D came out to her parents. Until that time, she had been open and honest about herself with her parents regarding the rest of her life. However, she became increasingly troubled and guilty about the fact that she knew she was a lesbian but had not shared that part of her life with them. Debbie D thought remaining closeted would only cause her to grow further apart from her family. She was unsure and afraid of their reaction; she knew from living with them that they were uneducated about the gay population. Debbie D knew, however, that she needed to tell her parents and believed that they had the right to know their daughter fully. They also had a right to their reaction to her revelation, whatever that reaction might be. She believed that because she knew her parents were straight, they too had a right to know that their daughter was lesbian.

Debbie D's parents were the first people she came out to. Coming out for the first time represents the beginning of the fourth stage of coming out. Here, the smaller inner circle is repositioned again by moving slightly through the circumference lines of the middle circle and the largest outer circle. As a result of the repositioning, three overlapping circles are formed (see Figure 4). The location of the smaller inner circle to the middle and outer circles represents gay and lesbian adolescents coming out and moving even further away from homophobic and heterosexist beliefs. It also represents gay and lesbian people acquiring more gay pride, gay education, and contacts with gay people and gay advocates than in the previous stages. At

FIGURE 4

The Fourth Stage of Coming Out Represented by Three Overlapping Circles

The first coming-out experience occurs during this stage. There is continued movement away from heterosexism and toward increased gay education and pride.

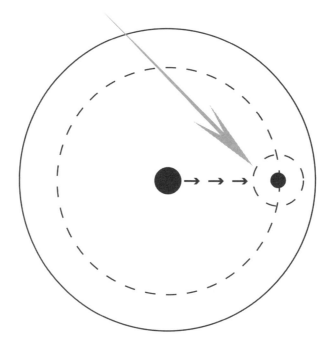

the same time, gay and lesbian people are less influenced by the bombardment of antigay education.

Debbie D's mother and father were accepting of her when she came out to them. While supportive of her, they were also distraught over the news. Debbie D was distraught over their reaction, imagining they loved her less. They were upset because they too were raised in a prejudicial and discriminatory society. They too feared the cruelty she might face because of her lesbian identity. They held the false belief that, because their daughter was lesbian, they would never experience her getting married, having children, and having grandchildren. Debbie D's parents found themselves in a situation where, while they loved their daughter, they were uneducated about lesbian issues and lifestyles and had no idea where to obtain the education in order to help and better understand their daughter.

Debbie D had known about her lesbianism for years and had time to cope with the knowledge of her sexual identity. Her parents, on the other hand, heard the news of their daughter being a lesbian for the first time when Debbie D came out to them and needed time to process the news. Their initial reaction was one of acceptance while simultaneously being filled with shock and fear. Their initial reaction served as verification that heterosexist and homophobic education was successfully instilled in them from childhood as well. They too were indoctrinated by their parents, peers, and media and by educational, religious, and political systems to fear gay people. Debbie D realized that both she and her parents were born into the same heterosexist and homophobic society that indoctrinates people at a time when they are not yet at the stage of mental maturity to have the option to reject or accept that knowledge. Subsequently, people do not know that they are prejudiced or discriminatory until after they already are.

Debbie D and her family exemplified the typical heterosexist and homophobic American family traveling the path from prejudice to pride. Continued travel on the path is not a given. Heterosexist and homophobic family members who do nothing to decrease their prejudice or increase their gay education when a gay family member comes out to them do not continue traveling along the path from prejudice to pride beyond this point. Their hopes of gay enlightenment are thwarted, with little hope for advancement in their understanding and acceptance of the gay family member and the gay population. At the same time, like all individuals, they are not static, and therefore, it is safe to say that their levels of heterosexism and homophobia will only increase as long as there are no efforts made to decrease them.

What causes some people and not others to travel the prejudice-to-pride path?

Some of the factors involved in whether or not gay enlightenment will be pursued and achieved are: (1) how often heterosexist people are exposed to enlightened gay people in order to be educated by them; (2) whether or not people's heterosexist views are confronted by others; and (3) how open, honest, pliant, dissatisfied, and empathetic heterosexist people are when confronted with their own prejudice and discrimination. A heterosexist individual can only change from prejudice to pride if they come in contact with, and are willing to interact with, and be reeducated by gay advocates and gay people. A heterosexist individual can only change from prejudice to pride if they eventually realize and acknowledge their prejudices and admit the falseness of their beliefs. The more people who can be reeducated and befriend those discriminated against, the deeper the pride, and the lower the prejudice and discrimination believed and manifested.

Proud gay and straight people possess various levels of education and are on different parts of the path from prejudice to pride. Pride is a spectrum of different rays of insight. It is measured by intensity, depth, and expanse. The experiences promoting gay pride are as numerous and individualistic as a person's fingerprints. There can be relapses and regression. Gay pride is not achieved without episodes of dissatisfaction, suffering, motivation, and bliss. Usually, the deeper the pride, the deeper the attraction will be to continued education and growth.

After coming out to her parents, Debbie D began interacting more with the gay population but not without continued fear, prejudice, and hesitation. The fear, prejudice, and hesitation stemmed from the effects of her heterosexist rearing and because she still hadn't received adequate gay education and gay interactions. In time, however, Debbie D developed many friendships with other gay and lesbian people because she was open to associating with the community and finding her place in it. The openness was verification that society's heterosexist and homophobic teachings were not insurmountable. In fact, for Debbie D, befriending and being reeducated by gay and lesbian individuals were the two major factors that enabled her to disprove the validity of the heterosexist myths she was raised with. She became angry, distrustful, and dissatisfied with mainstream society, feeling that she was lied to about the gay population. She wondered what else she was misled about in her upbringing. As a result, her anger, distrust, and discomfort led her to temporarily dissociate from the majority and only associate with gay people.

The act of segregating oneself completely from the majority and only keeping the company of gay people represents the beginning of the fifth stage of coming out. Stages 4 through 7 are post-coming-out stages. The fifth stage is depicted again by three concentric circles, where the smaller inner circle has moved completely into the outer largest circle, representing the self-imposed segregation of gay people from mainstream society (see Figure 5). Some gay people remain at stage five for the rest of their lives because they have great difficulty overcoming their distrust, anger, and dissatisfaction with their family of origin, religious groups, and heterosexist friends. They do not return to or participate in mainstream society. They only associate with other gay people and gay advocates because they are more comfortable with and trusting of this population. Many gay men and lesbians, however, only remain segregated from mainstream society temporarily. They put in the hard work to understand and decrease the anger, mistrust, and dissatisfaction to one day reenter and fully participate in, and with mainstream society.

As time passed, Debbie D realized that dissociating herself from the majority was not wise or fair to mainstream society, and maintaining that level of anger and mistrust was not conducive to living a healthy and rewarding life. She unfairly and unwisely discriminated against the entire

FIGURE 5

The Fifth Stage of Coming Out Represented by Three Concentric Circles

This stage represents the self-imposed segregation of gay and lesbian individuals from mainstream society.

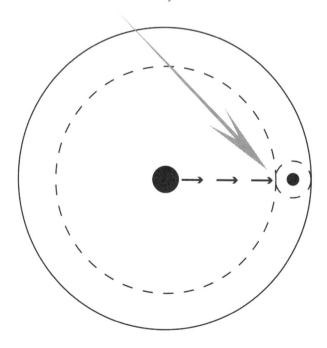

majority of the population, when not every person making up the majority was discriminatory. She realized that this type of behavior was akin to the mindset of the heterosexist people who discriminated against her because of her sexual identity.

Heterosexist people need gay role models like her to help disprove their heterosexist and homophobic notions and to reeducate them. Subsequently, Debbie D readjusted her priorities by realistically living in both communities. She became a lawyer and has helped play an influential role in advocacy for the LGBTQ populations.

The reuniting of the gay person with the heterosexist majority represents the beginning of the sixth stage of coming out. This stage is depicted by three overlapping circles (see Figure 6). The inner smaller circle represents gay people obtaining continued gay education and having found a healthier way to live by repositioning themselves mostly inside and partly outside the outer largest circle. In this way, gay people have the option, at any given

FIGURE 6

The Sixth Stage of Coming Out Represented by Three Overlapping Circles

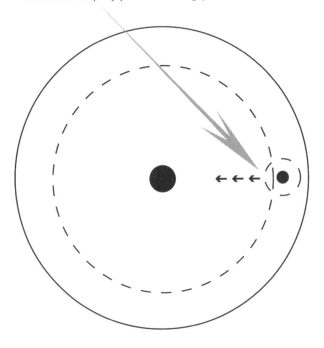

This stage represents the reuniting of the gay person with the heterosexist majority post continued gay education.

point in time, to participate with only the mainstream, with gay people and the mainstream together or with only other gay people.

The seventh stage of coming out depicts gay people who have reached gay enlightenment. This stage includes gay and lesbian educators, activists, and advocates. The three circles in stage 7 are depicted as overlapping as they are in stage 6 (see Figure 7). The difference in the positioning of the three sets of circles in stages 6 and 7 is that in stage 7, gay men and lesbians consciously, continuously, and intentionally position the inner smaller circle's location in reference to the middle and largest outer circles' locations through the application of increased knowledge and experience. These efforts ultimately afford and reward gay people with the highest attainable levels of comfort, benefits, confidence, pride, and satisfaction.

It is important to note that travel through the stages is fluid, rather than static, and can be continuously readjusted with conscious efforts. For example, one can approach stage 5 of coming out, experience horrific

FIGURE 7

The Seventh Stage of Coming Out Represented by Three Overlapping Circles

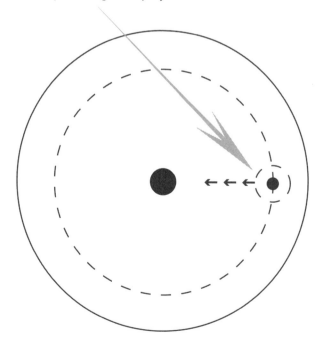

This stage includes gay and lesbian educators, advocates and activists consciously educating the majority.

discrimination from another, and relapse to an earlier stage. Gay men and lesbians can also skip certain stages. For example, some gay men and lesbians never enter or travel through stage 5. They skip from stage 4 to stage 6. Sadly, fewer gay men and lesbians reach the seventh stage of coming out than most gay educators and advocates would hope for. Those working in stage 7 are much like diamonds that have reached a state of perfection, with the ability to continue to enhance their lives in every way.

The path from prejudice to pride is never simple or easy, but the knowledge gained from the experience can transform a person. Only after Debbie D traveled the path and experienced the stages of coming out was she able to fulfill her dreams and passion to become a lawyer and gay advocate. While traveling on the path, Debbie D learned about the negative energy ripples contained within prejudice, homophobia, heterosexism, discrimination, and oppression and the positive energy ripples contained within gay advocacy, support, higher self-esteem, and self-care. She gained knowledge and experience about the falseness of the negative energy ripples and the damage they cause and the truth about the positive energy ripples and their productive effects.

Years of academic education and genuine gay education yielded a lesbian professional lawyer equipped with the understanding of the important role education plays in lifting the population from the trenches of homophobia and heterosexism to the heights of gay advocacy, equality, safety, and pride.

CHAPTER 7

Prejudice to Pride

Prejudice to pride is a journey delineating past to present travel of gay men and lesbians as individuals, as a community, and on levels, be they personal, familial, educational, legal, political, or religious. The individual journey reflects how gay men and lesbians progressed psychosocially from living in fear, depression, and distrust to living with self-respect, self-esteem, and pride in community. The community journey reveals the many ways that gay men and lesbians have helped themselves and the majority move away from heterosexism and homophobia toward gay equality. *Prejudice to Pride* emerged with every intention of reaching at least one person waiting, wanting, and willing to know more about the path and using the book as a guide to facilitate that travel.

Most people usually think in terms of dichotomies rather than specific percentages when labeling someone as prejudiced or enlightened. Most people group themselves and others into binary boxes of extremes: prejudiced or not prejudiced, proud or not proud. This all-or-nothing approach fails to grasp the complexities of human thoughts and feelings; that rather than consisting of certain amounts of prejudice and certain amounts of pride. People actually run the spectrum of prejudice to pride, sometimes being more prejudiced or less prejudiced, and sometimes being more or less proud, depending upon the incident, the interaction, and the level of openness, empathy, gay education, heterosexist background, and understanding.

People's prejudices and pride can and do advance, regress, and relapse. When prejudice increases, pride decreases, and vice versa. For example, there are many people who relate stories of how they were once more prejudiced than present day. The combination of social experiences with gay people and gay education, however, helped these same prejudiced people lessen their prejudice and increase their pride. There are those, such as newborn babies, who have no prejudice at all against gay people but become prejudiced by way of heterosexist education. Some people are unaware of their prejudices. They often deny the claim and say they feel no prejudice toward others. Then, there are those who were once more proud, but the burden of discrimination and antigay education diminished that pride and left shame in its place.

It is safe to say that states of prejudice and pride are fluid rather than static. Each will vary to greater or lesser degrees according to personal levels of experience and education. This chapter is devoted to describing the path of travel from prejudice to pride and from heterosexism and homophobia to gay education and enlightenment, in alignment with the seven stages of coming out.

During the first two stages of the coming-out process, gay men and lesbians acquire heterosexist and homophobic education from their family of origin and society. By stage 2, the influence of heterosexism and homophobia on gay men and lesbians is at its peak while levels of gay pride and gay education are virtually nonexistent.

In stage 3, gay men and lesbians are still prejudiced against gay people but with a glimmer of budding gay self-pride. Gay education and social contacts begin during this stage, albeit in small amounts. The amount of antigay education received is still very high during this time, but the influence of heterosexist and homophobic education is lessening. Stage 3 of the process also finds a slight increase in pride.

What made Debbie D more prejudiced in stages 1 and 2 was being raised in a heterosexist and homophobic society. She was inculcated with prejudice in the formative years, before she matured cognitively and emotionally, which made it easy to proselytize her. In addition, she had little or no known exposure to gay people and gay education until her adolescent years.

During the latter part of the fourth stage, for Debbie, this was during her late teenage years, and her curiosity equaled her fear of the gay microculture. She ventured out to a lesbian bar to help prove or disprove the myths and stereotypes that she had been taught regarding gay men and lesbians.

Upon first entering the lesbian bar, Debbie D found herself in the company of lesbians who, until that point, were still very foreign to her upbringing and social environment. For example, this was the first time she was in a bar comprising only women. It was almost impossible for her to view the lesbians in the bar without prejudice because Debbie D could not put aside the heterosexism or homophobia she was raised with. The lesbians' company, behavior, communications, postures, and culture were alien to her.

Although Debbie D did not know what to expect before visiting the lesbian bar, she surely did not anticipate such a variant experience. In the bar, she could not discern whether the stereotypes about lesbians were right or wrong. She was excited to finally confront the lesbian microculture even though she felt confused and frightened by the experience. Even though Debbie D's level of prejudice against gay people was still high in the fourth stage, at the same time, it was lower than in the prior three stages, and lessening all the time. Her level of gay pride had increased, as exhibited by her openness to visiting the lesbian bar, where the opportunity for education was high.

Debbie D's level of gay education increased during the fourth stage by interacting with other gay people. While the influx of antigay education did not decrease during the fourth stage, Debbie D's belief in heterosexism and homophobia did, along with the influence both had over her. It took several years of interacting with lesbians before Debbie D began to understand the lesbian microculture and to further decrease her own prejudice toward lesbian and gay people.

The effects of heterosexism and homophobia on the gay microculture make it exceptionally hard for people to come out. In retrospect, Debbie D found it miraculous that she, or any gay person, ever decides to come out because the path from prejudice to pride is painfully difficult, hard to travel, and definitely not based on a "choice" to be gay. Only a heterosexist person who does not know or has not experienced the gay microculture could believe such an erroneous statement that being gay is chosen or preferred. You will not find a gay person holding such a belief.

Who is in a better position to be accurate about whether being gay is inborn or chosen? Is the openly gay person with personal gay knowledge and experience better believed? Or is the heterosexist person, who is less familiar with the gay microculture and more influenced by heterosexist education, to be trusted? The answer is quite simple: A gay person is much more equipped to weigh in on this issue. This too, is why gay people learn about real gay life from gay-friendly people and not from heterosexist people.

Heterosexist people are less equipped with the knowledge and experience of the gay microculture. This is especially evident when, for example, we look at the heterosexist education straight people have provided society through the present day. Perhaps, from now on only people who are truly educated on the gay microculture should provide research and education on the matter. Heterosexist people need to understand that the sexual education they have provided thus far has been discriminatory, very damaging, and misinformed to say the least, and needs to stop. Let's hope that one day the stereotypes and bias will be eradicated and everyone will become gay educated.

While gay people do not choose to be gay, many of them choose when, where, how, why, and to whom they come out. Many out gay people choose to take the path from prejudice to pride. Many out gay people choose to increase gay education and decrease gay prejudices. Many out gay people choose to educate others to do the same. Openly gay people choose the suffering that goes along with coming out. They choose to enhance and expand their gay education in order to increase their quality of life and safety. Many out gay people choose to make efforts that will gain equality and protection. They choose openness and bliss over isolation and depression. They choose life over suicide, praise over denigration, and education over ignorance. Many out gay people choose to help raise the collective consciousness of the country to help gain gay pride in the minds and hearts of all.

The pride Debbie D feels as a lesbian was gained through personal growth and the positive, mutually educational relationships she found on her path. It is also due to her understanding the inequities and cruelties imposed on gay people and the wrongness of both. In some ways, however, the depths of the pride Debbie D is capable of feeling are directly connected to the level of pride the country feels for its gay citizens. For example, Debbie D's level of gay pride will increase from its current level when gay people gain legal equality, such as the legal right to collect social security benefits upon the death of a spouse. Her level of gay pride will expand when gay people gain the legal right to marry and receive employee-based health insurance for their partners and families and when she knows that heterosexist people no longer discriminate against gay people. Her level of gay pride will swell when we demand equal rights for all people, including gay people.

It is often said that everyone and everything is connected, that one person's gain is a gain for all and that a loss for one is a loss for all. That which is defined as a *gain* is that which benefits and supports all people and does not hurt them. That which is defined as a *loss* is that which discriminates against some people and hurts all people in the process. The sooner all people realize the truth in this statement, the sooner the planet will be able to recover from these illnesses of prejudice, discrimination, and oppression.

Illnesses that lead to murder, subjugation, segregation, suppression, and gay bashing will cease to exist. Doing away with these illnesses will lead to a healthier, more balanced and loving society.

What causes gay people to suffer while traveling along the path from prejudice to pride? As previously discussed, many gay people suffer as children and teenagers when the primary support systems are prejudiced towards gay people. Gay people suffer when they are rejected and abandoned by their homophobic families and have to build new support systems. This can be an extremely difficult time in a person's life and cause an enormous amount of stress. Many gay people become depressed and isolated during this time and suffer with lower self-esteem. Alcohol and drug problems often start, with increased incidences of suicide ideation and act, homelessness, school dropout rates, HIV status, and gay bashing.

Some gay people never develop a new support system after being abandoned by their families and, as a result, suffer for a lifetime. It can take years to rebuild support systems, and the suffering remains constant due to experiences of discrimination, lack of equal rights, painful coming-out experiences, problems with remaining closeted, lowered self-esteem, and trust issues. Gay people face these issues about their sexual identity day in and day out. These thoughts and feelings help color each day.

The majority of people segregate gay people through the use of active heterosexism and homophobia. As a result, many gay people temporarily stop interacting with mainstream society and begin to only interact with the gay world in order to cut off the feelings of abuse and prejudice perpetrated by heterosexist society. In other words, gay people set up a type of respite care for self-healing. Ironically, some gay people also are prejudiced toward other gay people during this time because they have not yet totally dispelled the prejudices that they too were taught by the majority about the gay microculture.

At this point on the spectrum from prejudice to pride, the level of prejudice against gay people is definitely lower, and self-pride is higher than in the prior four stages. Stage 5 also reveals gay people with less heterosexist and homophobic influences, and increased gay education, than at any other point of the previous four stages.

Interestingly enough, at this stage, many gay people begin to feel more prejudice toward the heterosexual community. For this reason, gay people begin to identify with and seek solace in the gay community, with efforts to build new support systems based on honesty, trust, understanding, and empathy.

It is not an easy task for a gay person to work on relinquishing prejudices toward the gay microculture and themselves. Nor is it easy for a gay person to work on relinquishing prejudices toward their family and friends, the educational and religious systems, and peers that lied to and discriminated against them. This is a "sink-or-swim" time for gay people. Nevertheless, many gay people somehow survive this sinking feeling until they learn to swim. Part of the sinking feeling comes from isolation and self-segregation. Another part of the sinking feeling comes from holding on to prejudice and intolerance toward all people, gay or straight. Finally, part of the sinking feeling comes from the continued discrimination felt from the majority and from family and friends.

Most gay people eventually realize that the way to avoid sinking and begin swimming is to acknowledge and forgive prejudices, in order to swim in both worlds. It can take many years, even a lifetime for a gay person to travel the path to the point where they have embraced the gay community and still participate in both the gay and straight worlds. Subsequently, once this level is attained, gay people gain bicultural status by beginning to healthily assimilate into and embrace both the gay world and the world of the majority.

At this point on the journey from prejudice to pride, a person entering the sixth and seventh stages has crossed the bridge from prejudice to pride and feels more pride for gay people and less prejudice toward heterosexist people. This feeling is called true gay pride or the beginning of gay enlightenment, and it reflects healthy, empathetic, and supportive feelings for self and for all. This stage also represents the highest levels of gay education and the lowest regard for heterosexism and homophobia.

A person who has reached the sixth and seventh stages of coming out has debunked the majority of heterosexist myths; befriended other gay people and gay advocates; acquired more gay education and gay pride than in the previous five stages; segregated from the mainstream due to anger, distrust, and dissatisfaction with it; reunited with the mainstream after relinquishing their distrust, dissatisfaction, and anger with the mainstream; and participated as healthy contributors to both the gay community and mainstream society.

The value that support systems contribute to healthy living, I believe, is often underestimated because there is too little communication and education about it, especially in childhood. Without caring and nurturing support systems, people grow up to exhibit a decreased ability to care for, trust, and nurture themselves and others. Consequently, isolation, depression, and lowered self-esteem develop, which hinder the ability to develop self-care: a social life, job, hobby, intimate relationships, passion, and motivation. With this kind of vicious cycle, gay people who lack a healthy support system find it difficult to cultivate the skills needed to develop a support system, which in turn, prevents the unhealthy life from becoming healthy.

In order to lead a healthy productive life, a trusted support system is crucial. Gay people differ from others in marginal groups in that many are forced out and abandoned by their families and must find a new network of support.

Debbie D related her experiences of the years she spent on this part of the path. Her life felt surreal when she began distancing herself from family and friends. She experienced the grief, loss, and bereavement one feels when a loved one dies. There was an odd feeling of being reborn onto foreign land while never having moved to a new location. She was startled and depressed. There was a sense of living upside down, and she didn't know how to return her feet to solid ground. There was no one to talk with or receive help from about the problem, because there was no support system. She knew that creating a new support system could offer hope and encouragement. Debbie D decided to take a chance by reaching out and trusting that confiding in another person would lead to the start of a truly healthy relationship.

If a gay person can overcome the fear of being rejected by coming out, the chance of developing a support system increases. In fact, two ways for an openly gay person to develop a support system are: (1) entering into therapeutic treatment; and (2) developing at least one loving, caring, and supportive friendship or relationship. This type of foundation will provide the gay person with the coping skills needed to work on grief, loss, and bereavement and will help provide the momentum to continue developing relationships with new individuals and groups.

Many gay people that feel depressed and isolated will eventually return to the world of the majority and their family of origin to help restore relationships and live productively. They might go back to school, get jobs, join clubs, support the gay movement, develop hobbies, have social lives, vacation, or raise families. In time, the gay person will see the world right side up again by developing a healthy support system and becoming an active and valued citizen.

Once gay people cross the bridge from prejudice to pride, they need to educate and encourage the majority to cross the bridge too. The pride that gay people feel can only increase to a certain level unless the majority of people begin work to increase their feelings of pride toward the gay micro-culture. Without the majority of people advocating for gay people, the statistics will continue to reflect a lack of equality, support, and rights.

When gay people are prohibited from marrying, the pride and dignity they fight for is diminished. If gay people are subjected to hate crimes and gay bashing without protection under the law, their level of pride will be dampened. If gay people are prohibited from adopting children and gaining employee-based health insurance for their partners and families, their level of pride will surely be weakened. If a gay person's pride is devalued, then those who cause this problem will suffer too. There is no way to separate the discriminator from the one who feels discriminated against. If gay people are subjugated by the majority, and the majority does nothing to rectify the problem, then human civility is at risk of disintegrating.

Gay people everywhere should attain the level of self-pride that encourages openness and honesty and serves to educate the majority about gay life, issues, and pride. In order for gay people to continue advancing toward equality, they must understand the importance of educating the majority about the misinformation and dishonesty of heterosexism and homophobia, and why and how the hate and fear must end. Gay people cannot ignore discrimination. Instead, discrimination must be addressed through empathetic means to change the current levels of ignorance and fear. Subsequently, pride within, and for all, will increase in more people's hearts.

Only when homophobia and heterosexism are forgotten and replaced with pride will our nation enact laws to establish and protect gay equality. The term *gay tolerance* will become obsolete because it will reflect the bygone, discriminating culture of the past. For now, the term can be used as a gauge for how far American culture has advanced from past levels of discrimination until present time. Extremely hot days are tolerated; sickness is tolerated; not earning a salary while attending graduate school is tolerated. Negative things, people, and situations are tolerated. Being gay is not negative or shameful. Gay people should not be viewed in a negative light or simply tolerated. Rather, gay people should be accepted, supported, and included with society.

More time spent thinking of ways to increase equality and decrease heterosexism will result in more pride, enlightenment, and satisfaction. The more gay people come out and serve as role models, the greater the number of people there will be to educate straight and closeted gay people about the gay community, and the greater the likelihood that the gay population will become genuinely known and visible rather than falsely imagined by the majority. When all people are educated about real gay life and people, the advancements made toward equality, respect, and civility will be felt by all.

CHAPTER 8

Homophobic Religious Leaders and Members

Certain religious groups are the main supporters of gay oppression. Religious leaders and followers exhibit hypocritical behavior when preaching love, honor, and respect while simultaneously excommunicating and ostracizing people from the congregation on the basis of their sexual identity. You cannot expect your lesbian and gay family members to believe with their whole hearts that you love them completely and unconditionally when you support a group that hates gay people. If the rationalization is that you hate the sin (or the gay act) and not the sinner then, anyone can say they love everyone and simultaneously rationalize their hate. Why hate the sexual act of love between two people with a gay sexual identity? This is definitely not the belief of a truly religious person.

If you belong to a religion that denigrates gay people and you are a parent of a gay person who claims to love and support your child, then you are being hypocritical, whether or not you realize it and whether you support the discriminating aspect of the religion or not. A true supporter of gay equality would have no affiliation with a religious group that denigrates gay people. If you believe that gay people should not be allowed to marry because the Bible says so, then you are mistaken. Nowhere in the Bible does it say that marriage is the right of only a man and a woman. This belief is man-made. Love is not meant for only some and not others. Do unto others as you would have them do unto you is not a phrase that came with a list of exceptions; nor did it come with the understanding that you can treat people any way you want and expect nothing but love in return.

There are many who use the religion card to condone gay discrimination. There are many people who hate and discriminate against the gay population while justifying it by saying that God deemed gay people immoral. There is no foundation for truth in the message. Many people consider their religious beliefs and behaviors necessary and plausible. In reality, these denigrating beliefs only prompt the statistics on gay hate crimes and crimes of violence to soar.

Proposition 8 was a ballot initiative and constitutional amendment that was presented in November 2008 to voters in the state of California. This amendment would overturn previous efforts to allow same-sex couples to wed. Many religious groups who oppose gay equality helped pass Proposition 8 in California by investing money to advertise and gather support for their cause. This support shows a prime example of the lack of separation between church and state and the conflict that can result. The United States needs to fulfill its promise of equality for all by offering equal protection to its gay citizens. The United States needs to address the fact that everyone has the right to be protected and share in equality and that the gay population is excluded from these rights.

In order for any progress to be made in this area, the United States government needs to limit the authority and influence exerted by certain discriminatory groups. Religious groups have a right to believe whatever they wish. However, religious groups do not have the right to influence legislation based on their view of morality.

Discriminatory religious organizations should expect that gay people will continue to educate their heterosexual family members about the hypocrisy and disadvantages to belonging to these types of groups. Religious leaders can count on more gay-enlightened people addressing the issue of churches using tax-exempt state and federal government dollars and property to proselytize their members to demoralize gay people. This issue is not going away. A time will come when heterosexual and gay people alike will demand change. One hopes that in time religious groups will reflect love, equality, and inclusion and reject discrimination and hatred.

Religious leaders who continue with their discriminatory ways will find themselves abandoned by heterosexuals and closeted gay people because their flock will see the light of love and gay education, which does not include discrimination against anyone. New churches are forming and will continue to form that consist of people who believe in equality and fairness for all people and who won't tolerate injustice and discrimination.

So deep are the hypocrisy and discrimination in certain segments of the Catholic and Christian churches that coalitions have been formed that seek to prevent and hinder gay rights. Support for gay equality is increasing with each year, so it stands to reason that more and more people will be unwilling and unable to cope with the hypocrisy and hatred spewed from homophobic religious organizations. If church leaders don't find a way to tone down the rhetoric of hatred and exclusion, it is very likely that they will lose support and people will go in search of churches and congregations that offer love, support, and respect.

The term "religious war" has existed throughout history. The term has earned the irrefutable, chronic, and real reputation for connecting religion with war, which is a far cry from the ideals purported by religious organizations. Religious organizations should be judged based on reality rather than their ideals. In reality, no one can love and hate at the same time. However, certain religious groups have been killing in the name of love for centuries. This hypocrisy, coercion, abuse of power, and hatred must be stopped. Never again should God's name be used to accomplish the act of hate and murder, all in the name of love and religion.

How many lives have been lost in vain in these religious wars? The answer is too many. How many more people must suffer and die before religious organizations are called to account for their wrongful deeds? How long will it take before people realize that far too many innocent lives have been lost to hate? When will gay people stop being ostracized from their families because their parents, siblings, friends, teachers, employers, and coworkers falsely believe what their religious leaders taught them? Religious leaders hold positions of power in the community, and it is time for them to stop teaching their followers that gay people are sick and demented sinners. When will family members support and love each other instead of accepting those who preach hate and offer false quotes from the man-made Old and New Testaments, Koran, Torah, and other religious books in the name of love? When will honest and truthful education begin?

Life is full of ironies. For example, are the closeted sexual acts of nuns and priests who take vows of celibacy considered sinful? The answer is yes, according to the Catholic Church, because God knows and sees everything regardless of the hidden nature of the acts and because the nuns and priests knowingly sinned by breaking their vows and lying about them. The irony is that these nuns and priests are not punished, and they remain members of the church while honest, openly gay parishioners who have done nothing wrong are condemned and excommunicated. Is there one set of religious laws for the clergy and another set of laws for the congregation?

Who would associate with a gay person after learning from religious leaders that the gay sexual acts (that are found out) are sinful but not the actual gay person? It's a rather confusing message. People are not going to separate the act from the sinner. It stands to reason that many people will still believe that there is something sick or depraved about someone whose "acts" are believed to be sick and depraved. They will either unconsciously or consciously hate the gay person as well as the act. The proof of this is witnessed in everyday life. The real question should be: Who would want to be part of a religious group that believes irrational, hateful beliefs and behaves in unloving ways? The answer should be no one. Hopefully someday, no one will.

Those religious leaders who teach hatred and intolerance are wrong, sinful, and sick. They have helped produce a society of people, including gay people, who hate both gay people and the act of homosexuality. This result, I believe, was the real intent of religious leaders all along and a prime example of subtle, under-the-radar type of discrimination. Furthermore, even closeted, celibate people know deep in their hearts that they are still gay, even if they have never had sex with another person of the same gender. Choosing to be celibate does not change the fact that they are gay or lesbian. Another long-held fallacy and example of heterosexist homophobia is the singular focus of making gay people out to be only sexual people and defining them solely by the sexual act.

Being gay is as much mental, emotional, social, economic, legal, biological, educational, sensual, spiritual, and religious as it is sexual. In other words, if every gay person on this planet stopped having sex, then there still would be the same amount of gay people on the planet. The problem, in part, stems from homophobic religious leaders promoting ill and Draconian attitudes toward sex and sexual identity. Then, they link the attitudes with gay discrimination in order to successfully demoralize and ostracize the population.

I remember two years ago an incident of discrimination that occurred on the job. A gay couple was given an engagement party by their coworkers. Two of the born-again Christian coworkers declined the invitation because they said that their religion did not support gay marriage. Therefore, it would be a sin for them to attend the event. However, when another gay coworker's father died, the same two coworkers who did not attend the engagement party attended the funeral. This event, they said, had nothing to do with the gay sexual act. The agency where these people worked was a not-for-profit Orthodox Jewish agency. This agency acknowledged the gay marriage and said that they would not allow the one gay worker to supervise his gay partner because married partners cannot be in a supervisor/supervisee relationship as this would represent a conflict of interest.

However, one partner could not reap the benefits of the other partner's employee-based health insurance because the gay marriage was not truly acknowledged by the agency. The gay couple could not tolerate this discrimination and responded by resigning from the agency. They found jobs in Chicago with higher status and pay and with an agency that would not tolerate sexual discrimination. Subsequently, the discriminating agency suffered by losing two brilliant workers.

Why support a religion that has no knowledge of or experience with the people it condemns and ostracizes? Why support a religion that condemns gay people and, at the same time, supports and pays the salaries of its own numerous closeted gay priests, nuns, rabbis, and ministers? Why support religious groups who condemn gay people and support the "don't ask, don't tell" policy? Religion is big business. It is a business that does not pay taxes and simultaneously helps prevent gay people from receiving the benefits that gay taxes pay for. Imagine a not-for-profit organization whose mission statement espouses love, hope, faith, charity, patience, and respect while simultaneously influencing state and federal policies to increase the hate, slander, abuse, and murder of innocent gay people.

The "don't ask, don't tell" policy has been active not only in the military but all throughout society; in families, schools, workplaces, and the social, political, and religious arenas, from childhood on through older adult years. It is a policy that has crippled civilization, and it's full harmful effect still isn't truly known. Does heterosexist society have any idea of the price paid by closeted gay people for living according to the "don't ask, don't tell" policy? Out people would surely suffer less if gay population statistics represented the full community of gay people. Heterosexuals could abandon the ridiculous notion that the entire population would turn gay if gay people were given their equal rights. This same ridiculous notion helps verify that homophobia and heterosexism are personality disorders and acknowledge the list of psychosocial/gender/sexual problems that come from heterosexism and homophobia and that could be treated with psychosocial counseling.

There are still not enough heterosexuals actively seeking education about gay people. Even though there is at least one gay person in every family, heterosexuals still do not show enough of an active interest in listening to their gay family member(s) or obtaining gay knowledge from the educational systems, books, magazines, journals, or seminars. This fact exemplifies how successful this country has been in indoctrinating its citizens with homophobic education in a way that helps prevent its citizens from motivating themselves to seek real education about the gay community in order to dispel their homophobia.

In the past, white people discriminated against black people by advocating that black people were inferior. White people supported segregation between the two groups. White people used the religion card in order to justify and enforce the discrimination. White people used the religion card to enforce discrimination against Jewish people as well. Playing the religion card was very successful in conditioning white people to believe that Black and Jewish people were evil and inferior. The result of the discrimination was the needless suffering and deaths of many black and Jewish people because of the ignorance of white people.

Today, many heterosexist black, Asian, Hispanic, Mexican, and Jewish people support gay discrimination with the use of the religion card. When viewed in light of the discriminatory religious groups, it is not very hard to believe that some of the same people who have dealt with prejudice and discrimination in the past are now choosing to continue with the bigotry by targeting gay people. What enables many of them to discriminate against gay people is, I believe, unconscious and aided by the use of the defense mechanism, "identification with the aggressor." What this means is simple. Those who have been discriminated against have been abused. Victims of abusive experiences learn to become victims, abusers, or both.

Those who identify with the discriminator, or abuser, sometimes discriminate and abuse others, just as they were abused. Such is the case with Jewish or black people who have known discrimination but who now discriminate against gay people. This is a type of personality disorder that needs to be acknowledged and addressed by parents, teachers, and therapists everywhere.

The true hypocrisy is evident when you consider the famous religious teaching, do unto others as you would have them do unto you. Yet bigotry and hatred are tolerated when it comes to homosexuality. There are many religious black, Jewish, Asian, Hispanic, and Mexican people who will do anything to help their family members and friends when discriminated against because of their color, or ethnicity, or religion; yet they will not protect their gay family members when discriminated against because of their sexual identity. They even actively and personally take part in discriminating against their own family members because they are gay. The reason for the discrimination is, in part, due to the heterosexist and homophobic education provided to them by the religious organizations.

The sad truth is that society verifies it is ill when gay people all over the country watch their rights taken away by means of the majority's homophobia and discrimination. Gay and lesbian people must help reeducate those heterosexist individuals from minority groups to realize the atrocity of their actions. Gay and lesbian people will help stop the murder, hate, and abuse, justified and cloaked in the name of religion and God. Gay and lesbian people will help turn this planet around and make it a safe, loving, and healthy place to live for gay people, and for all people.

I have had countless experiences with other minorities who considered me to be an immoral sinner because I am lesbian and because their religion taught them this. It is amazing that these same people do not accept discrimination lashed out against them and do not realize their contrary beliefs and behaviors. At the same time, they will defend religions that depict gay people as perverted and evil pariahs to be condemned for their sexual identity. People should really get to know the people that they discriminate against instead of blindly believing the falseness of the stereotypes.

What is unfathomable is that people who discriminate against gay people are the very same people who do not know or who are not educated on gay people and yet vote on issues that prevent gay people from being afforded their legal rights. These same uneducated, heterosexist people are the voters deciding the fate of gay people. These discriminatory voters have no place voting on whether or not another citizen should be denied their rights because discrimination should be considered illegal. In the land of the free and equal, it is unconscionable that this struggle and the denial of rights even exist. It is shear lunacy that gay American citizens are fighting for rights that should be freely given. It is absurd that people are completely conditioned to ignore this fact and that uneducated, discriminatory people have a vote in who receives protection and equality from the government.

What about those people who claim to support gay rights, with the exception of legalizing gay marriage? That is the equivalent of saying that a person can be "pro-women" with the exception that he believes that women should not have the right to vote. Or someone who claims to not discriminate against black people yet, in the same breath, believes that black people should not be allowed to drink from the same water fountain as white people.

When some of the people prevent others from access to their legal rights, then everyone suffers a loss of dignity, safety, and equality. The act should be acknowledged as illegal, and the perpetrator as criminal. Such is the case in New York, where the lesbian and gay population thought that New York would have been the first state to legalize gay marriage. Now, New York's reputation for being a liberal state has been restored after passage of the same-sex marriage law. However, many gay New Yorkers will never forget their frustration during that period when several attempts to pass the same-sex marriage law failed. It was during that same time that a number of gay New Yorkers moved or planned to move to those states that had already legalized same-sex marriage. After all, why live in a state that denies part of its community its rights, dignity, safety, and civility when you can live in a state that acknowledges respect, equality, protection, and support for the gay community and the entire population?

I wish the reader to understand that I am not anti-God. I am suspect, however, of religious organizations whose words and deeds hurt and damage people's lives. Nowhere in the Bible, Koran, or Torah does it mention the word *church* or *synagogue*. Religious organizations are man-made organizations that act as spokespeople for God. In reality, God never instructed religious organizations to thrive. In reality, religious organizations are big, money-making companies with tremendous political influence.

I believe in God, where God is depicted as all loving. I believe that all Gods believed in are one God. I do not, however, believe in a God who hates and condemns gay men and lesbians. I do not believe in the kind of organized religion that professes to love all and, at the same time, denigrates some of its members. I do not support religious groups that depict a God who would deem the gay population to be sinners, evil, and perverted while simultaneously depicting their religious groups as all loving.

I consider myself religious and spiritual. I believe in God being composed of loving energy and found in everyone and everything. I believe in miracles. I believe that the reason we were all put on earth is to create, develop, and love each other. I believe in religions that reflect this love in God, in each other, and in themselves. I believe in and support religions that accept and embrace gay people made in God's image. I believe in religious people who do not accept or tolerate gay discrimination and, instead, actively denounce all discrimination. I believe in and support people who embrace a God who would never tolerate unfairness and inequality. I believe in gay-supportive religious people helping to reeducate those who discriminate against the gay community. I believe God to be an all-loving God, one who does not turn against people or love them any less because of their gender, color, race, age, religion, ethnicity, sexual identity, or mental status. This then, would not be God. Instead, it would represent the falsely devised myths created by those who created religious organizations to hold worldly political influence, collect billions of tax-exempt dollars, and decide who is worthy of justice and God's love. For the sake of everyone's continued health, civility, and growth, this negative portrayal of God needs to be rejected.

CHAPTER 9

Church and Conservative Right-Wing Enmeshment

I t is interesting to note that while gay people fight for the legal right to marry, many did not know, until the resurgence of this fight, that marriage affords over 300 state rights and over 1,100 federal rights. Gay couples are denied all of these rights. Whether straight couples marry through the church, city hall, or both, the religious or civil marriage is legally acknowledged on the federal and state levels. The marriage of heterosexual couples is acknowledged in all of the United States, in every country, and by every religion.

As of 2009, gay marriage and divorce in the United States are only legally acknowledged in Washington, DC, and in six states. The rest of the United States denies gay men and lesbians the right to marry on the state and federal levels. Gay couples gain more than 300 state rights through marriage but only in the states of Vermont, Massachusetts, Connecticut, New Hampshire, Iowa, and New York and in the District of Columbia. Gay marriage was initially legalized in California and Maine but was eventually overturned in November 2008 and November 2009, respectively. Gay couples are denied over 1,100 federal rights in all 50 states. Worldwide, gay marriage is not acknowledged in the majority of countries. Gay marriage is denied by the major religions throughout the United States. Gay couples interested in marrying under God in a place of worship, and in the few states that acknowledge gay marriage, must look for a gay-friendly place of worship and an officiant who is an advocate of gay marriage.

All religious groups allow straight couples the right to marry in every country. Certain religious groups such as the Christian right, Mormons, Catholics, Jews, Jehovah's Witnesses, and Muslims support the denial of gay people's right to marry in the United States because they believe that God denounces gay people and that marriage is between only a man and a woman. Therefore, these religious organizations and conservative right-wing groups are hugely responsible for supporting the exclusion of gay people from more than 1,400 rights that marriage affords to heterosexuals only. The efforts made on the part of these religious organizations and conservative right-wing groups to continue to deny gay people the rights accompanying marriage reflect what I call church and state enmeshment.

Many religious orders have tax-exempt status because they act as non-profit businesses and intend goodwill. With this tax-exempt status, the government is not supposed to interfere with how the religious organizations operate. Likewise, religious organizations that have tax-exempt status are not supposed to interfere with government operations by engaging in partisan political activity or by endorsing or campaigning for or against a political candidate. If religious orders do interfere with government operations in this way, then this is considered unlawful and tax-exempt status will be rescinded.

One such incident of possible unlawful influence of church on government affairs was discovered when a Catholic bishop tried to influence the voters in Brooklyn, New York, by making a barrage of phone calls to them prior to elections. During the phone calls, the bishop endorsed a Democratic candidate who was a major player in defeating a bill that would allow victims of child abuse to file suit years after the alleged incident.

It is a well known fact that the Catholic Church has been rocked by allegations of child sexual abuse. Clearly, a bishop who works in an organization that has been accused of horrid crimes of abuse against children should not use his influence to get voters to interfere with the punishment for such crimes. Naturally, the efforts on the part of the bishop were to help prevent: (1) the continuance of present lawsuits against the Catholic Church for alleged crimes that occurred years ago; (2) government interference with alleged illegal acts of the church; and (3) the potential loss of millions, if not billions, of dollars to the lawsuits involving the alleged abuse. This alleged illegal act of partisan campaigning on the part of bishop was a blatant one.

The religious clergy definitely used large amounts of tax-exempt monies to influence the citizens who voted to overturn legalized gay marriage in California and Maine. Although these acts did not directly influence, support, or endorse politicians' votes, they directly influenced the citizens' votes, which directly influenced the votes of the politicians by overturning their previous votes that legalized gay marriage in California and Maine. Therefore, religious organizational monies influenced the politicians who legalized gay marriage by squelching or quashing their voice once it had spoken. Either way, religious organizations influenced politicians, political issues, citizens, and government laws and used semantics to get away with it while not losing their tax-exempt status.

The way that the existing laws are written fosters discrimination because the laws were written by religious heterosexist people, in heterosexist times, and in heterosexist environments. The work that lies ahead in changing these heterosexist laws will take time to change. Meanwhile, gay people everywhere continue to suffer from the effects of these heterosexist laws while living in a country that falsely claims to be loving, free, and equal for all.

The Mormon Church spent a huge amount of money to help overturn Proposition 8 in California, thereby denying gay people the right to marry after previous laws allowed it. This act of influencing the voters through fear tactics enabled many more people to understand that the church has been influencing state and federal laws regarding gay marriage for centuries and has played a dominant role in the denial of gay people's legal rights up through the present time. This realization also represents hundreds of years of people ignoring gay people's lack of rights and equality. Consequently, forward progress for the gay movement has been painfully slow.

One way to ensure that antigay religious organizations will not be able to impose their morality on others is for people to boycott these discriminatory organizations. A second way is to allow all gay people the right to a civil marriage. In this way, all citizens could legally enjoy the rights and benefits that come with marriage. Religious groups would no longer be able to influence the denial of federal and state rights granted to gay people in the arena of a court. Individual religious groups, however, would still have the right to decide whether gay men and lesbians will be accepted into, and can marry within, their religious group. Religious groups would have the right to do this (until laws are enacted that label this act as discrimination and illegal). In this way, church and state will be separate and equal. Gay people will gain the more than 1,400 rights accompanying civil marriage and will begin reaping the benefits that straight married couples have been enjoying all along (and which gay citizen's taxes have helped pay for, for years).

Federal and state laws treat married straight couples differently than gay couples. Gay couples are considered business partners and are deemed the equivalent of strangers according to the way the laws are written on partner benefits. Many gay people find out later in life about the inequities existing in the laws on the inheritance or estate tax, social security benefits, and 401(k) benefits for gay couples. Why is there no education provided on these laws related to gay people? The answer is simple. Most straight parents and families are ignorant when it comes to this information because it does not pertain to their lives. Therefore, the information is not sought after, taught, known, promoted, or passed down from generation to generation.

Lack of education, discrimination, heterosexism, and homophobia all are contributing factors causing the lack of available information on the denial of gay rights. This leads many gay people to deal with the economic and legal inequities pertaining to their lives when it is too late. It is crucial that gay individuals learn this type of information as early on as possible to protest the discrimination and to formulate plans on how to best secure these particular aspects of one's life.

When a married heterosexual couple shares equal ownership of all monies, properties, and assets, and plans to leave their half of the assets to the surviving spouse, the spouse inherits everything after the death of the other spouse, and legally does not pay any taxes on any of the inheritance. When a gay couple shares equal ownership of all monies, properties, and assets, and each leaves their half of everything to their partner, the surviving partner inherits everything and pays taxes on all inheritance over a certain amount. These same inheritance laws that pertain to gay couples exist for strangers and business partners. It should not be the case that when a gay partner dies, the surviving partner then must pay inheritance or estate tax. This means that the surviving gay partner is being taxed twice for all monies, assets, and properties.

Gay people should begin to receive all of the benefits that straight people receive. To level the economic playing field, either everyone should have to pay an inheritance tax or no one should. In no way, however, should only the gay community continue to be financially penalized. This economic discrimination must end.

Until 2008, married heterosexuals who inherited a retirement savings plan could roll those savings over to an individual retirement account (IRA) and pay no taxes on the inheritance. Married heterosexual couples also inherit social security benefits without any tax penalty. Gay couples, on the other hand, have always been denied social security and survivor benefits.

It was not until the latter part of 2008 that President Bush passed a law allowing employers the option to let their employees' nonspouse beneficiaries roll over inherited retirement benefits to an IRA to avoid immediate taxation. The law was passed granting this benefit to all nonspouse beneficiaries, including gay partners.

While the passage of that law reflects tremendous gains for gay rights, it did little in the way of exposing the centuries of oppression gay couples have tolerated. In other words, when this law was passed, there was no acknowledgement that, until this time, the laws denied gay people their rights and the laws were unjust. There was no statement made that this law was passed as a response to gay oppression and meant to help rectify the hundreds of years of unfair treatment with regard to survivor benefits. There were no apologies made. Furthermore, the law states that this benefit is optional and that individual companies can decide to allow it or not. If they opt to not incorporate the measure, then gay people will continue to suffer from unfair inheritance policies.

Religious, conservative, right-wing leaders paid millions of dollars to ensure that Proposition 8 passed in California while neglecting to spend a penny on addressing the skyrocketing divorce rates in their congregations. It seems like a wasted opportunity to deal with serious issues instead of continuing the mean-spirited, bigoted fight to deny equality.

The majority of funding that helped put Proposition 8 on the ballot and pass it came from the Mormon Church's donations to the Focus on the Family Ministry; from the Knights of Columbus, which is the Catholic Church's Connecticut-based political support group; and from private donors. Religious leaders should not have the right to use tax-exempt state government dollars to exercise their power and influence to change state laws and votes. Also, people write off millions of tax dollars donated to religious organizations, which are used to influence politics. Major religious organizations that oppose gay people's equality and rights must be careful of congregational mutiny.

Divorce rates are much lower in the more liberal northern states and much higher in the more conservative southern states. Some gay people are wary of marriage for romantic reasons. This truth is evident in the high level of divorce rates and in the lack of heterosexual spousal role models that would inspire gay people to consider marriage for romantic reasons. One of the main reasons most gay people want the right to marry is for legal and economic reasons—that is, to obtain the over 1,400 rights that accompany marriage. Many of these rights entail economic protection for the spouses, children, monies, properties and assets.

Marriage is a broken institution that needs fixing, as demonstrated by the high divorce rates. This problem is widely ignored. Why would gay people want to enter into an institution that reflects the level of problems that marriage does? Gay people want the legal and economic protection provided by marriage. Some gay people want to be blessed by God in their marriages. Some gay people view marriage as romantic and want to experience this feeling. However, gay people do not want the burden of discrimination that comes from being denied equality.

Those gay people marrying soon after passage of the same-sex marriage law differ from heterosexual people in their histories of knowledge and experience with marriage in certain important ways. Heterosexual people grow up with the option to marry. Many also desire to marry. More often than not, heterosexual people marry within a few years of meeting each other. From their childhood on through adulthood, there is a building of desire and excitement in planning for the happy day, always with a freedom to do so. A number of heterosexual people do not focus on or even know many of the laws protecting them through marriage.

Until passage of the same-sex marriage law, gay people did not grow up with the option to marry, even if they desired it. Many gay couples who are currently marrying have been fiancées for numerous years. They too are happy and excited to tie the knot. But the history that accompanies them to the marriage ceremony is one of having struggled and fought for years for the right. At the same time, they always considered themselves married during the years they shared together in love. Marriage for gay couples represents the legal legitimacy of the marriage and the gaining of the protection of laws already learned and previously denied. Gay people are not seeking the rites of the sacrament from the Catholic religion or the bar/bat mitzvah ceremony from the Jewish religion. Gay people are not seeking a religious rite from a religious group. Gay people are seeking a legal right, that is, the right to marry on the city, state, and federal level. This right is not a religious right. It is a civil and legal right, which should be automatic and granted through entitlement as it is with heterosexuals. It should not be interfered with, blocked, or prevented by religious groups. This is a civil and legal right that should not have to be approved by religious leaders and groups who have aggressively worked to deny gay people the right to marry. Political and legal leaders should step in to acknowledge, stop, and right this oppressive wrong. Marriage is older than religious groups and not solely owned by religious groups. The denial of the civil right to marry reflects a serious criminal problem in the culture of all people and must be recognized as such.

PAST TO PRESENT VIEWS

CHAPTER 10

Heterosexism, Heterocentrism, Homophobia, and the *DSM*

The terms "heterosexism," "homophobia," and "heterocentrism" origi-
nate from the prevalent and persistent oppression against gay people;
a newly deepened gay vision resulting from increased unity; an unwill-
ingness to accept prejudice and discrimination any longer; and recognizing,
addressing, understanding, defining, describing, and labeling the causes of
discrimination more accurately and specifically. *Heterosexism* refers to the
stigmatization, hatred, demoralization, discrimination, and prohibition of
any sexual identity outside of heterosexual identity. *Homophobia* is defined
as an irrational hatred, disapproval, or fear of homosexuals or their culture.
Heterosexism causes homophobia. Homophobia fuels and sustains heterosexism. Each feeds off the other and helps increase discrimination against
and prejudice toward gay people.

Gay men and lesbians need to continue expanding the glossary of terms
that define this prejudiced mentality. The creation of additional vocabulary
will reflect current gay life. It will help reorient mainstream society to see
from new perspectives both the progress made and the horrible mistreat-
ment felt by the gay community. Gay men and lesbians need to increase
gay education and help all people to see that heterosexism and homophobia are characterological problems.

A third term, heterocentrism, or falsely imagining that opposite-sex attraction is the best, and the only right and sane identity, joins the terms heterosexism and homophobia to form a triad of interacting beliefs and behaviors that have kept oppression alive. Heterocentrism, not homosexuality, should be viewed as hostile and damaging. Discrimination, not homosexuality, should be studied for its unhealthy symptoms. It is important to understand that the behaviors of the majority are not automatically the norm, or sane, legal, and healthy, as was verified by, for example, the tragic events of the holocaust and the atrocious institution of slavery.

In 1952, homosexuality was labeled a mental disorder in the first edition of the *Diagnostic and Statistical Manual of Mental Disorders (DSM)*. Nearly 35 years later, in 1987, homosexuality was removed from the *DSM-III* and no longer considered a mental disorder. It is my contention that the labeling of homosexuality as a mental illness evolved in two ways: (1) The numerous mental and emotional symptoms that led to the diagnosis of mental illness in gay men and lesbians were linked with toxic heterosexist, homophobic, and heterocentric causes; and (2) the psychiatrists who labeled homosexuality as a mental illness did so in part, through heterosexist, homophobic, and heterocentric environmental influences.

In 1952, there were lower levels of gay and lesbian support and higher levels of heterosexism, homophobia, and heterocentrism. Psychiatrists who were largely influenced by the cultural climate and social environment labeled homosexuality a mental disorder. By 1987, there were higher levels of gay and lesbian advocacy and lower levels of heterosexism, homophobia, and heterocentrism. Psychiatrists again influenced by the cultural climate and social environment, removed homosexuality from the *DSM*, and no longer considered it a mental disorder.

The ratio of discrimination to advocacy in 1952 and 1987 undeniably helped determine whether or not gay men and lesbians were considered mentally ill. It is easy to understand that what caused increased cognitive, emotional, behavioral, and spiritual problems in gay men and lesbians in 1952 were reflections of higher levels of heterosexism and homophobia and lower levels of support and protection. Conversely, it is just as easy to understand that what caused decreased cognitive, emotional, behavioral, and spiritual problems in gay people in 1987 were, in fact, reflections of lower levels of heterosexism and homophobia and higher levels of advocacy and protection.

When psychiatrists first defined homosexuality in the *DSM* as a mental disorder, they did not mention in their psychiatric evaluations that gay and lesbian mental illness originated predominantly from environmental causes rather than from their innate sexual identity. During this time, psychiatrists did not realize that their professional psychiatric evaluations of gay men and lesbians were distorted by the projection of their own heterosexist and homophobic personal judgments onto their gay and lesbian clients. These same irrational judgments put forth by psychiatrists were molded by the influences of the discriminatory society in which they were raised. The majority of society then adopted this distortion by labeling the entire gay and lesbian population as mentally ill. An apology to gay men and lesbians everywhere for these atrocities is crucial to future healing.

The damage done to the gay population by classifying homosexuality as a mental disorder in the *DSM* for over 35 years is incomprehensible and overwhelming. The extensive list of problems gay men and lesbians internalized as a result of the discriminating psychological, religious, educational, and political worldview on homosexuality is staggering: family hatred and abandonment, sexual abuse and disease, homelessness, school dropouts, suicide ideation and acts, gay bashing, hate crimes and crimes of violence, alcohol and drug problems, depression, isolation, lowered self-esteem, anxiety, distrust, paranoia, shame, loneliness, invisibility, and victimization due to the lack of civil and equal rights; lack of property, insurance, estate, adoption, and employment rights; and use of the religion card to help maintain discrimination against gay people.

Heterosexist, heterocentric, and homophobic beliefs and acts contain negative energy ripples (see chapter 13) that, when emitted, are transferred to and internalized by all of society. This type of negative and uneducated energy originates in heterosexist, heterocentric, and homophobic people, not in homosexuals. The discrimination and prejudices are continuous, pervasive, and ever destructive, not only for the gay and lesbian victims but also for the aggressors as well.

The perversion and mental, emotional, and behavioral disorders projected onto the gay and lesbian population actually exist within the minds, hearts, and actions of those who discriminate, not those who are discriminated against. Currently, the worldview is still upside down in seeing homosexuality, rather than discrimination, heterosexism, and homophobia, as personality and paranoid disorders. Laws must be enacted that label heterosexism, homophobia, and discrimination as criminal acts in order to shift the worldview to right side up and accurate.

Gay people, more often than not, begin to experience discrimination within the family of origin. Marginal groups that are discriminated against—such as black people, Jewish people, Asians, Muslims, American Indians, Hispanics, people with mental illness, and people who are intellectually and physically challenged—have the support of their family to battle and cope with discrimination. They do not experience discrimination from within the family. Rather, they share and pass down ways to cope with and respond to discrimination.

Heterosexist families do not equip their gay and lesbian children, siblings, parents, and extended families with the necessary knowledge to battle societal discrimination. Instead, heterosexist families align themselves with society by exercising prejudice and discrimination against their own children, or other family members. Gay people are taught few coping and defense mechanisms as children to buffer and help prevent the damage caused by the heterosexism and homophobia inflicted on them by the family of origin and society.

Gay men and lesbians often share a history of being debased or disowned by their homophobic family of origin instead of being supported or protected. Some families make it unbearable for the child to remain living at home and leave the gay child no recourse but to eventually run away. This traumatic form of abuse suffered by gay men and lesbians often requires psychotherapy to treat the resulting mental, emotional, physical, and behavioral problems.

Society has certain aspects of the media, and religious, political, and educational systems to thank for the irrational fears planted in the minds of families causing them to irrationally inflict pain on and ostracize their loved ones simply because they are gay. Since heterosexism and homophobia were the primary contributing environmental factors causing the mental disorder in the gay person, it would be safe to say that heterosexism and homophobia should be looked into as personality and paranoid disorders. Individual family members should seek psychotherapeutic treatment for their heterosexist and homophobic defects which harm gay family members.

Heterosexism and homophobia are relatively new words that describe age-old irrational behaviors, fears, and attitudes. The amount of time it took for these two terms and their definitions to be created and recognized verifies the degree of entrenchment and suppression of gay and lesbian discrimination kept in place by the majority of society. The two terms *heterosexism* and *homophobia* are historical words in that they represent gay men and lesbians making strides in freeing themselves from suppression and a victim mentality; gaining strides in increased support, respect, and equality; and beginning to separate themselves from the discriminator to accurately and appropriately label them with personality and paranoid personalities.

The following assessment describes heterosexist and homophobic symptoms, which is the precursor to the labeling of such cognitions, emotions, and behaviors under the category of Axis II disorders. Heterosexist and homophobic people's cognitive, emotional, and behavioral development often are first arrested in childhood and adolescence, when their families and society at large first transmit vitriolic antigay education to them, which prevents healthy adult maturation. As a result, heterosexist and homophobic people first begin exhibiting borderline, paranoid, and antigay social personalities as early as childhood. They also possess lowered self-esteem, a bully mentality, and an inability to think logically or with sound judgment regarding gay people. These characterological patterns of problems prove to be fixed, enduring, and harmful to one's own personality, to gay men and lesbians, and to society as a whole. These same problems have ramifications in social, occupational, familial, educational, and religious areas of functioning, which help ensure that people do not question the accuracy of heterosexist and homophobic education.

People who are discriminatory possess bully mentalities and choose individuals whom they perceive as weaker than themselves to discriminate against. Therefore, it is no coincidence that minority groups and women are often targets of discrimination. Heterosexist and homophobic people exhibit symptoms of borderline personality by lacking self-trust and trust in others and by viewing people only from the perspective of the majority versus the minority. In other words, they see things negatively, in black and white, or in extremes. They do not see the spectrum of colors, that is, the view of all people as one and unified, with healthy similarities and differences. In addition, those heterosexist and homophobic people from minority groups join the majority mentality when discriminating against gay men and lesbians, thereby affording the minority groups the opportunity to be linked with the bullying majority, and avoid being the victim.

People with a bully mentality exhibit the symptom of lowered self-esteem. Heterosexist people need to believe that they are better than gay people and that gay people are not as good as them. Naturally, this distorted view stems from heterosexist people trying to compensate for their own lack of self-worth by bullying gay people. Heterosexist people with a bully mentality exhibit antisocial symptoms by not associating with or befriending gay people. This fact represents a lack of developed social skills and the inability to accept differences as well as similarities among the majority and minorities. People with a bully mentality exhibit narcissism. Heterocentric people hold the false and irrational belief that their sexual identity is always the only right and normal one. Naturally, they also believe that any sexual identity outside of theirs is abnormal, perverted, and evil.

People with a bully mentality exhibit aggressive rather than empathetic attitudes and feelings. This symptom often stems from heterosexist people's history of having been victims of abuse themselves. It originates from oppressive heterosexist education passed down from ancestors, which contains abnormal, false, hateful, and aggressive views toward gay people. Consequently, those receiving the false and hateful education identify with the abusive educator (out of fear and lack of cognitive maturation needed to question or dismiss the erroneous beliefs), and begin abusing gay people. The bully mentality is sustained by the majority using their size to actively bully smaller and presumably weaker individuals and groups of people.

Heterosexism should be listed in the *DSM-IV-TR* as an Axis II personality disorder. Homophobia should be listed in the *DSM-IV-TR* as an Axis II paranoid disorder. Taken together, the disorders describe people with chronic cognitive, emotional, and behavioral problems negatively affecting their personality and societal health. The disorders arise as early as childhood and evolve into enduring patterns of characterological deficiencies, including irrational fear, avoidance of others, low self-esteem, narcissism, problems with trust, and an overall lack of pleasure, present in adulthood. Heterosexist people project their own distorted, irrational, and aggressive attitudes and fears onto gay people, and then believe these fallacies about gay people to be true. Heterosexist people are unaware of their symptoms, which is a symptom itself, and much harder to treat. This type of unawareness makes the therapist's work much more difficult, especially if the therapist is also heterosexist and homophobic.

Heterosexism and homophobia are responsible for the protuberance of statistics on hate and violent crimes against gay people. Those discriminating against gay people should be recognized not only for their personality and paranoid problems, but also for their criminal offenses as well. The intention of the use of prejudice and discrimination against all minority groups are similar across the board, that is, to subjugate, slander, and enslave. One way to help facilitate this understanding is through citing examples of prejudice and discrimination used against various minority groups, and exposing the irrational beliefs, fears, and similarities among them.

It cannot be denied that the atrocities inflicted on Jewish people during the holocaust, and on black people during slavery and through the period when civil rights were finally established, were reprehensible. Today, most people realize and admit that these types of slaughter and destruction were caused by ignorance, irrational fear, and discrimination. Most people today do not agree with the stereotypes that black people are ignorant, inferior to white people, or poor, lazy, criminal, and dangerous. Most people today do not agree that black people should sit in the back of the bus, drink from separate water fountains, or attend different schools than white people.

Most people today also do not agree with the stereotypes that Jewish people are thieves, frugal, conniving, dirty, and greedy. Instead, most people today realize and acknowledge that the ignorance and falseness of the demeaning statements made against black and Jewish people were falsely constructed to help maintain their subjugation, and were responsible for their murders. When will people realize and acknowledge that the intent behind the falseness and ignorance of the demeaning statements made against gay men and lesbians is the same as the intent behind the false and ignorant statements made against black and Jewish people, and for that matter, every other minority group who has felt the sting of discrimination.

Listed below are popular statements of stereotypes and acts of discrimination made by society's majority against gay men and lesbians. These statements and acts of discrimination will serve as examples of personality disorder expressions or criminal behavior. It is up to today's psychiatrists and the legal system to review this section carefully to begin the work of assessing and diagnosing heterosexism and homophobia as Axis II disorders, including gay men and lesbians in the laws that protect all people, and arresting those who commit harmful and violent acts of discrimination against gay people.

The first seven statements depict homophobia and are not only false but originated from and contain irrational fears:

1. Gay education should not be taught in the schools because these efforts would increase the chance that all people will turn gay.
2. Do not make contact with gay men for fear of contracting HIV or AIDS.
3. If gay people are allowed to marry, then the institution of marriage, as it has been known for centuries, would be obliterated.
4. Allowing your son to associate with gay people will put your son at risk for being molested and turning gay.
5. Gay people should not be allowed to donate blood or organs or society will be at risk for contracting HIV and AIDS.
6. A gay mother said that she would rather her son be paralyzed than gay.
7. The homophobic view contends that the minds of children will be corrupted if consent is given for gay education to be incorporated into the school system. Sadly, the message being sent here is that you can use the word *faggot* (acquired through homophobic education) but not the word *gay* (acquired through real gay education) in schools.

The next set of four statements exemplify heterosexist, heterocentric statements that are inaccurate and based on the belief that heterosexuality is the only right and normal sexual identity:

1. Homosexuality is sick, evil, sinful, immoral, and an abomination.
2. Marriage is meant for only a man and woman.
3. Gay people can unlearn their homosexuality and become heterosexual.
4. Homosexuality is a mental illness.

The next seven statements relate real and true acts of discrimination against gay people:

1. A man is beaten severely because he is gay.
2. A lesbian receives a dishonorable discharge from the army after coming out.
3. A lesbian is refused housing due to her sexual identity status.
4. A gay man is excommunicated from the Catholic Church because of his sexual identity.
5. A gay couple is refused the right to marry.
6. Gay men were used as faggots or logs to burn the fires that killed the Jewish victims of the holocaust.
7. The parents of a gay son disowned him for being gay.

Further studies on heterosexist people will "out" their centuries of personality and paranoid disorders which have gone undiagnosed. Heterosexist people have a history of vacillating between not acknowledging gay men and lesbians for positive reasons and acknowledging gay men and lesbians for negative and punitive reasons. For example, heterosexist people use the invisibility syndrome, which serves the purpose of not providing laws that recognize, advocate, support, protect, and ensure equality for gay people. Such is the case in the military with the use of the "don't ask, don't tell policy," where the positive deeds done by gay men and lesbians to protect the country and its people are denied and then, if acknowledged, punished with dishonorable discharge. This type of paranoia and personality disorder needs to be recognized as such, addressed in all aspects of life, both public and private, and legally prohibited.

Some heterosexist people believe that gay people should not be allowed to marry and often use the following two reasons to justify their belief: (1) to protect the sanctity of marriage believed to be designed for being only between a man and a woman; and (2) to protect the children (from being raised by abnormal and perverted gay or lesbian parents). In this example, heterosexist people do not want gay men and lesbians to have the legal right to enter into the institution of marriage. In other words, same-sex couples are to be ignored by denying them the legal right to marry.

Heterosexist people, parents, and families negatively acknowledge gay men and lesbians by falsely imagining that gay marriage and gay parents will harm children in every aspect of their life. What actually harms children is heterosexism and discrimination, not the exposure to gay individuals. It is a known fact that, within heterosexist families, at least one in three gay children has had a suicide ideation or act during their teenage years. This suicide statistic verifies the harm done by heterosexist parents and society to their gay children. This suicide statistic confirms that the myth that children need to be protected from being raised by gay and lesbian parents is false. It also reflects a false projection on the part of heterosexist people, the very same people who are responsible for contributing to the gay teenage suicide statistic and doing irreparable damage to gay and lesbian youths through their heterosexist beliefs, teachings, and influence.

In addition to outright heterosexist people, there are many people who claim to support gay rights but who still possess discriminatory beliefs or attitudes. It should not be assumed that when people claim to support gay causes, they mean that their support is 100 percent. There are what I call, closeted heterosexist people who claim that they do not discriminate against gay people, but actually do. They either know that they discriminate and lie about it or are unconscious about their prejudices and acts of discrimination and deny both. These people should not be, but are, represented in the statistics as providing full gay support.

There are heterosexist people who say they support gay rights, with the exception of supporting gay people's right to marry. These people do not embody full supportiveness and should not be represented as such in the statistics. Others, such as homophobic business owners, claim to support gay rights but discriminate by not hiring gay people in their place of employment. Although these business owners may support gay rights in many areas, they should not be considered to be full advocates for gay rights because this would be an inaccurate representation of their gay support.

Those gay men and lesbians who pass as straight in society and are not able to be identified as gay can vouch for the innumerable times they experience heterosexist discrimination and prejudice from people who did not realize they were in the company of gay people and would not have committed the acts or made the statements had they known they were. Many of these heterosexist people are unconscious of the hurt and damage they cause. For these reasons, research studies' calculation of statistics on gay support should be carefully reassessed and gathered in order to ensure reliable and valid results.

Although it is good that the current level of discrimination against gay people is lower than ever before and that current lower levels verify increased support of gay people, it is still important to "out" and acknowledge the percentages of discrimination and support to realistically know where the problems and advocacy lie. It is important to "out" and acknowledge those who discriminate unknowingly and those who discriminate knowingly in order to address the problems and reeducate. Without decreased discrimination, there can be no increased advocacy. It is important as well to know and acknowledge those who advocate for gay men and lesbians to devote their energy to reeducating those who discriminate. Without increased advocacy, there can be no decreased discrimination.

CHAPTER 11

The Model of Change

The model of change is a form of self-counseling that describes, step by step, how people can help themselves to grow. The model is a guide for people to understand their conflicts by listing the pro and cons of their conflicts and the consequences of siding with either the pro or con side of their conflicts. It contains the components that propel and resist positive change and the actual way to change. This chapter explains the modus operandi of the model by including an example of how one man crossed the bridge from being heterosexist and homophobic to being supportive of gay people. Usually, a person feels a desire to change when he or she is dissatisfied. Dissatisfaction arises when a person is ambivalent or holds two conflicting attitudes that cannot be reconciled. The two conflicting attitudes are called attitude one, the pro-attitude, and attitude two, the con-attitude. To change, a person's dissatisfaction and discomfort must increase to a level high enough to cause a third attitude to arise from within. The third attitude is a two-pronged attitude. It is called attitude three, the mediator/catalyst attitude, which is the mediator for attitudes one and two; and the catalyst for change, which pushes through the result.

The mediator part of attitude three continuously weighs and reviews the pros and cons of attitudes one and two carefully. When it determines which of the two conflicting attitudes it agrees with, it converts into the catalyst part of attitude three. The catalyst part of attitude three contains all of the emotional energy, knowledge, and momentum of the mediator part of attitude three. The catalyst part of attitude three is responsible for pushing through either attitude one or attitude two as the result, depending on which of the two attitudes the mediator part of attitude three agreed with.

In the model of change, each of the three attitudes consists of emotional energy. Each of the three attitudes consists of knowledge and beliefs that are acquired through internal and external influences. All three attitudes must be present and must interact in order for change to come about. If only one or two attitudes interact, and the third attitude is absent and not operating, then change will not occur. Far too often, people with the best intentions fail to succeed in changing because they do not use all three attitudes needed for change to occur. When people only use two attitudes to bring about change, the two attitudes continuously argue without the necessary energy to move forward and fail to produce a result. The following scenario is an example of how the model of change works.

Initially, John, a heterosexual and heterosexist man, only knew prejudice and discrimination toward gay people. John's heterosexist attitude was acquired from the education of a heterosexist family and society. He supported heterosexism in his everyday beliefs and actions. His heterosexism was considered attitude one, the pro-heterosexist attitude. What then caused conflict and the possibility of change in John?

John started to become dissatisfied with his prejudices of gay people after meeting and becoming friends with gay people. During this time, he began developing attitude two, the con-heterosexist attitude, which resulted from his supporting the newly factual gay education acquired through gay friendships and which disagreed with attitude one.

Eventually, John felt uncomfortable with the two contradictory attitudes and wanted the internal arguing to stop. He realized that his family, friends, teachers, and Christian religious leaders supported his pro-heterosexist attitude, which was in direct opposition to his gay friends who supported his con-heterosexist, or pro-gay side.

The inner conflict could only be resolved if and when attitude three, the mediator/catalyst attitude came into play as a result of attitudes one and two continuously arguing. Some of the reasons why attitude three might not develop are: (1) John may not be aware that attitudes one and two need that conflict with each other in order to work on producing a third attitude that will help resolve the struggle; (2) John may be too frightened to continue approaching the problem and regress to the state of denial and avoidance; (3) John may be aware of the dissonance and not want to work on and resolve it; or (4) John may be inexperienced in resolving conflicts. If attitude three does not develop for any of the reasons listed, then John will continue to live in either discomfort and discord or in denial that there is a problem by possibly terminating friendships with his gay friends.

As time passed, John continued to keep the company of the heterosexist people who supported his pro-heterosexist side (or attitude one) and the gay friends who supported his con-heterosexist side (or attitude two). He began to separately weigh and review the pros and cons of each attitude (one and two) in an effort to relieve the mounting frustration and dissatisfaction caused by the two attitudes constantly clashing and to gain insight into the problem. Then, he weighed and reviewed the pros and cons of the two attitudes taken together for the same reasons. The work that John did by listening to, weighing, and reviewing the pros and cons of attitudes one and two represents the mediator part separately then together, of attitude three actively employed and performing its function.

First, John weighed and reviewed the pros and cons of attitude one, the pro-heterosexist attitude. One of the many examples of pros and cons John weighed and reviewed was as follows: John stated that one of the benefits of being heterosexist was that he felt comfortable in the company of his heterosexist family, friends, teachers, and religious leaders who taught him the beliefs he held about gay people. Being heterosexist also enabled John to continue to normalize his sexual identity, and label gay people as abnormal and deviant. On the other hand, John related that one of the drawbacks of being heterosexist was that he felt uncomfortable holding heterosexist beliefs in the company of his newly acquired gay friends and gay education. He found that the stereotypes prevented him from developing closer relationships with his gay friends because the beliefs he held about gay people were derogatory and segregating.

Second, John weighed and reviewed the pros and cons of attitude two, the con-heterosexist attitude. One of the many examples of pros and cons John weighed and reviewed was as follows: John stated that one of the benefits of renouncing heterosexism was that he felt equally loving and respectful of gay and heterosexual people. He found that he could move forward with the friendships with his gay friends because of his newly acquired gay education. However, John related the drawback of abandoning his heterosexism was the fear that he would either reject or be rejected by family, friends, teachers, and religious leaders. He also feared opposing their heterosexist beliefs because they might degrade him, and even consider him to be gay.

Third, John weighed and reviewed the pros and cons of attitudes one and two together. Several of the many examples of pros and cons John weighed were as follows. (1) John began to see that the knowledge he gained from spending time with his new gay friends disproved the myths learned in his childhood about gay people. This is an example of knowledge supporting attitude two, the con-heterosexist attitude, over attitude one, the pro-heterosexist attitude: (2) John was taught by his religious leaders to believe that gay people were evil, immoral, and perverted. John disproved this stereotype by seeing that his new gay friends were quite the opposite. They were polite, friendly, level-headed, good, and ethical people. This is an example of knowledge supporting attitude two, the con-heterosexist attitude, over attitude one, the pro-heterosexist attitude: (3) John was taught by his heterosexist friends that gay men were effeminate. On the contrary, John found a number of his gay male friends to be very masculine, muscular, and athletic. John said that he would have never known they were gay unless they came out to him. This is an example of knowledge supporting attitude two, the con-heterosexist attitude, over attitude one, the pro-heterosexist attitude: (4) John's family taught him that gay people should not be allowed to have children because, as parents, they would corrupt the children. In reality, John found his gay friends to be excellent parents raising happy, intelligent, and well-adjusted children. This is an example of facts supporting attitude two, the con-heterosexist attitude, over attitude one, the pro-heterosexist attitude; (5) John learned from his schoolmates that gay people were sexual deviants and that being gay was learned and chosen. John learned from direct contact with his gay friends that they were sexually healthy, well adjusted, and born gay. This is an example of truth supporting attitude two, the con-heterosexist attitude, over attitude one, the pro-heterosexist attitude: (6) John witnessed some of his female heterosexual friends blatantly exhibiting heterosexism by saying that, on the one hand, they did not want to know whether or not a person was gay. They insisted that a person's sexual identity was not anyone's business. On the other hand, these same women complained about boyfriends not revealing their bisexual or gay identity to their girlfriends, which, they said, put the girlfriends at an increased risk for contracting HIV. These types of contradictory and heterosexist statements too helped educate John to support attitude two over attitude one.

The mediator part of attitude three emerged from within John when his conflict arose. John mediated the pros and cons of attitudes one and two for as long as it took to develop the necessary levels of emotion, knowledge, and momentum required to decide which of the two attitudes he agreed with, which, in this case, was attitude two, the con-heterosexist attitude. This decision triggered the conversion of the mediator part into the catalyst part of attitude three. Subsequently, the catalyst part of attitude three performed its function by acting as the catalyst to push through attitude two, the con-heterosexist attitude, as the result. Consequently, John resolved the conflict and continued traveling on the gay-friendly path.

John erased the problem through reason, common sense, empathy, honesty, healthy ego function, good judgment, and weighing and reviewing the consequences of movement in both pro- and antigay directions. He now lives as a gay advocate and helps educate his family and friends on the reality and truth about gay people. He is relieved of his frustration, dissatisfaction, and discomfort caused by the conflict that arose from the discord between attitudes one and two. He no longer struggles with the dilemma of whether or not gay people are good or evil, ethical or unscrupulous, perverted or healthy.

John spent many years developing and resolving the problem. As a child, he automatically believed without question the heterosexist and homophobic education taught to him by his family, teachers, friends, and religious leaders. As a teenager, John started becoming friends with gay people, whose education disputed the heterosexist and homophobic education. It wasn't until John was 30 that he resolved the conflict and started living as a gay advocate. His years of consistent inner work, passion, empathy, humility, and patience eventually led to his increased happiness, productivity, peace, self-esteem, and consciousness.

The model of change should be introduced to those who are interested in solving inner conflicts and making positive changes. It is to be used as an added aid whenever someone wants to work on giving up unhealthy habits and on increasing mental, emotional, behavioral, spiritual, and physical health to promote increased quality of life. The model of change will alter consciousness and conscience by deepening and expanding both, provided one is ready to grow.

CHAPTER 12

New Glossary of Terms

Why are there labels, such as heterosexism and homophobia, to define and describe antigay people but no labels that represent people who were heterosexist, then acquired gay education, and rose above their heterosexism to achieve gay-educated and advocacy status? Although the creation of the two terms was insightful and brilliant, it appears there is more focus on labeling prejudiced and discriminating people, and their beliefs and behaviors, than on labeling educated advocates and gay innovative thinkers and their beliefs and behaviors.

This chapter includes a glossary of terms created by the author that will identify, define, and describe that part of the increasing population that has, through obtaining gay education and experience, transitioned from being heterosexist and homophobic to supporting the gay population. The glossary of terms originates from following the model of change's path from prejudice to pride and gay enlightenment. The glossary also contains newly created terms that are more inclusive of current attitudes toward sexual identity.

According to the model of change, heterosexist people only begin to want to change when they start feeling dissatisfied with their current beliefs and attitudes. The reason for the dissatisfaction stems from increased contact with gay people and gaining an honest education about the entire

97

community. People at this stage of gay educational growth develop two conflicting attitudes. Attitude one represents the *heterosexist dissatisfied*. Attitude two represents the *gay advocacy neophytes*.

The false heterosexist beliefs acquired from one's family of origin and society begin to clash with the newly acquired gay education and experiences. A state of unrest begins. If people continue to interact with gay people and receive this new education, then their dissatisfaction with their heterosexist attitudes and homophobia will rise. At the same time, their level of gay advocacy will rise. Naturally, tension and upset increase due to these contradictory attitudes.

People who continue to work toward resolution of the conflict begin to develop attitude three, or the mediator/catalyst attitude. At this stage of work, people are called the *heterosexist unsure,* representing attitude one, and *gay advocacy learners,* representing attitude two. These terms describe the increase in gay education and increase in dissatisfaction with heterosexist beliefs resulting from continued work on resolving the conflict.

The mediator part of attitude three converts to the catalyst part once people gather sufficient knowledge and experience to disprove their heterosexist beliefs and affirm the validity and reliability of their gay education. The catalyst part of attitude three pushes through the result, which is attitude two, and produces what I call the *gay advocacy thinker.* At this stage of the path, attitude one has been eliminated and is called the *debunked heterosexist.* Continued travel on the path from prejudice to pride naturally causes the continued increase of education about gay people and is represented by the terms *gay educators* and *gay enlightened.*

A person's identity is considered fluid and complex rather than static and dyadic. It is composed of social, familial, educational, economic, political, legal, spiritual, psychological, sexual, and psychic functions of living. For these reasons, it is not unusual that gay men and women are also attracted to members of the opposite sex and heterosexuals are also attracted to members of the same sex. It is human nature for people to be attracted to each other socially, psychologically, spiritually, politically, emotionally, and intellectually, without necessarily being attracted sexually.

Homophobia and the updated label, *gayphobia,* denote the irrational fear of gay people. I altered the term because today, most people identify more positively with the word *gay* than with the word *homosexual*. The reason for the two different connotations is simple. The word *gay* originated during a time when people were more pro-gay. On the other hand, the word *homosexual* evolved out of a more homophobic time and environment.

Gayphobia reflects irrational fear because it is solely based on stereotypes and myths and a lack of real gay education and contact. Consequently, some heterosexual gayphobic people exhibit increased levels of gayphobia when attracted mentally, socially, or emotionally to members of the same sex. The increase in fear in this particular kind of scenario is triggered by the irrational fear that they are gay, when in fact they are not. They mistakenly confuse social feelings for gay attraction, and they fear thinking of themselves as gay. This type of fear I label as *gaysocialphobia*.

Those who are opposed to heterosexism, gayphobia, and heterocentrism are what I call *anti-heterosexist, anti-gayphobic,* and *anti-heterocentrist* people. Those who support heterosexism, gayphobia, and heterocentrism are called *pro-heterosexist, pro-gayphobic,* and *pro-heterocentrist* people. Those who are pro-gay, I also termed *gayamorous*. Those who support gay and heterosexual equality are called *pro-gayheteroequality*. *Homomisia* means hatred of gay people. *Heteromisia* means hatred of heterosexuals. *Metrogay* is an urban gay individual. *Ruralgay* is a country gay person. *Advogayte* specifically means the support of the gay population, lifestyle, and individuals.

Other terms created to reflect today's level of gay support are *gay considerate* and *gay mindful*. These two labels describe people who do not automatically assume that everyone in their company is heterosexual. These two types of people are gayamorous (exhibit love for gay people), considerate, mindful, and respectful of gay people and acknowledge them as a valuable part of the population. The two terms represent people who release positive energy ripples to all and help increase gay and lesbian support, legal rights, and protection. These kinds of gay-friendly people are not in denial that gay people are their coworkers, friends, teachers, students, clients, therapists, family members, lawyers, store owners, and favorite actors, actresses, musicians, artists, designers, and athletes.

Terms such as *gay-innate* (born gay) and *hetero-innate* (born heterosexual) reflect the fact that people are born gay or straight rather than sexual identity being learned, chosen, or preferred. The term *heterosexist debunker* describes the kind of person who helps others disprove irrational fears about the gay population, and dismiss the false belief that only heterosexuals are normal and good people. *Heteropartial* refers to people who prefer to be in the company of heterosexuals. *Gaypartial* refers to people who prefer to be in the company of gay people.

The *heterosexist pseudo-religious* refer to people who discriminate against gay people by believing that God meant marriage to be between only a man and a woman; that heterosexuality is the only good and normal sexual identity; and that gay sexuality is evil, perverse, and to be condemned. The *pro-sexualvariance religious* refers to those genuinely religious or spiritual people who support the belief that all sexual identities are good and natural. These very same people imply that God supports all sexual identities.

Finally, the *sexual identity movement* is a term that describes people involved with the advocacy of all sexual identities as positive, healthy, and equal. *Sexual identity impermanence* is a term that refers to the fluid and transient nature of sexual identity. *Sexual identity gamut* is a term that defines the variety of sexual identities along the sexual identity spectrum. The new terms introduced for the first time in this book: *positive and negative energy ripples* (chapter 13), *gay enlightenment, the model of change* (chapter 11), and *prejudice-to-pride path* have also been defined. Hopefully, all of these terms, which were created in order to "out" the updated knowledge of the gay community, will help accelerate the gay movement in a positive direction.

CHAPTER 13

Positive and Negative Energy Ripples

Positive and negative energy ripples are a part of everyone's lives. Positive energy ripples exist within each person and help connect people through their love, trust, empathy, caring, and support for others. Negative energy ripples exist within each person and help disconnect people by way of ignorance, fear, lack of support and trust, lowered self-esteem, depression, guilt, prejudice, discrimination, and abuse.

Negative and positive energy ripples are carried within, between, and among people's words, emotions, thoughts, and behaviors. Negative energy ripples can rise to levels where they thwart people's baseline level of operation and ability to cope, causing healthy functioning to cease. If this occurs, outreach is needed in order for people to gain and help restore healthy functioning. On the other hand, increased positive energy ripples help increase every aspect of health and should be encouraged to proliferate.

Gay men and women experience discrimination from birth until death. When someone discriminates against a gay man or woman, negative energy ripples are emitted from the discriminator to the recipient of the discrimination, in this case, the gay person. Over time, some gay people begin to have difficulty coping because of the compounding effects of repeated experiences of discrimination. Consequently, negative energy increases and expands within the gay person's cognitive, emotional, behavioral, and

101

spiritual life, creating problems in each of these areas. If these problems persist, then the negative energy ripples expand to the gay person's social, medical, psychological, economic, educational, and legal life, creating problems in these areas as well. If this myriad of problems is not addressed, the negative energy ripples will continue to increase and begin to cause chronic damage in the gay person's life.

Jill, a 40-year-old artist, is a prime example of someone who has experienced negative energy ripples as a result of being discriminated against because of her lesbian identity. One day, Jill visited the hospital to donate blood. When the nurse handed her the blood donation form to complete, Jill read the form and quickly realized that she could not donate blood because gay people are legally prohibited from donating blood. Jill was shocked. She said that this experience was the straw that broke the camel's back.

As a teenager, Jill was abandoned by her family, church, and friends when she came out. Consequently, she isolated herself, was depressed, and experienced lowered self-esteem and problems with trust. Naturally, Jill's support system dwindled. She began having difficulties concentrating, which affected job performance. Eventually, problems with alcohol became evident. Jill, a part-time student, dropped out of college. Jill realized that she needed help coping. She reached out for help and was admitted to a detox and rehabilitation center for help with alcohol abuse. Then, she was treated at an outpatient psychotherapeutic clinic in order to address her problems and the accumulated negative energy ripples.

One year later, Jill's capacity to cope had greatly increased due to her positive response to rehabilitation and therapeutic treatment. She returned to work and school. She developed a new support system and was less depressed, alcohol free, more able to concentrate, and involved in a romantic relationship. As a result, Jill started to create and emit positive energy ripples. Jill had identified her problems, the triggers, solutions to the problems, her strengths, and the goals she wished to obtain.

Jill learned through counseling that the heterosexist and homophobic teachings she acquired were false. She learned that the acts of discrimination committed against her in the past played a key role in helping to increase her inability to cope. She learned that she must change her response to discrimination. She could no longer allow herself to identify with the aggressor (the discriminator). She learned to separate herself from the discriminator and develop increased defense and coping mechanisms. She could no longer take the negativity of the discriminator, which had rendered her unable to cope.

Jill began educating herself on how to address discrimination and the discriminator rather than reacting helplessly and allowing the negative energy ripples to cripple her. She understood that the negativity held within the one discriminating did not lie within her. She learned how to refrain from absorbing the negative ripple effects contained within the discriminator and discrimination aimed at her. She began responding, rather than reacting, to discriminators by educating them, which simultaneously sustained her own healthy functioning.

Negative energy ripples that exist within gay people stem from family abandonment; not being allowed to donate blood or organs; being denied social security benefits and having to pay inheritance tax upon the death of a partner; gay bashing; being denied employee-based health insurance for partners and children; being invisible due to being denied equal rights and protection under the law; religious subjugation and exclusion; being segregated; being denied the right to marry or divorce; increased alcohol and substance abuse used to help cope; the depression, lowered self-esteem, isolation, homelessness, harassment in school, and suicide ideation and acts resulting from prejudice and discrimination; the lack of psychotherapeutic gay-educated help needed to maintain good emotional health; remaining in the closet; the fear of coming and being out; being denied the right to adopt and foster children in most states; not reaping the benefits that gay and lesbian taxes pay for; employment and housing discrimination; heterosexist and homophobic teachings; being treated like pariahs when diagnosed with HIV/AIDS; the omnipresent "don't ask, don't tell policy"; and being denied respect and civility throughout life, even in older adult years.

Negative energy ripples aimed at gay people are found throughout history. The holocaust is a case in point, when overt and subliminal hatred toward gay men and lesbians manifested in needless murders. During the holocaust, gay men and lesbians were murdered simply because they were gay and lesbian. Symbols of pink triangles were created to count the gay murders. Black triangles were used to count the lesbian murders. Gay men were used as faggots, or logs, that fueled the fires to kill Jewish people during the holocaust. Hence, the derogatory term "faggot" was coined and passed down.

Today, many people use the word *faggot* in a derogatory manner, without knowledge of its origin or understanding of the pain it causes. Although the world knows of the atrocities that the Jewish population suffered during the holocaust, far fewer people know of the atrocities committed against the gay and lesbian population during that time. Oppression, gay and lesbian invisibility, lack of knowledge of gay history, and lack of laws representing gay and lesbian protection, safety, and equality are four reasons that the majority is unaware of these holocaust statistics. Those who deny that increased energy must be directed to reeducate the homophobic and heterosexist population represent proof of the dire need for reeducation.

DISCRIMINATION TO ADVOCACY

CHAPTER 14

Acknowledging the Harm
that Discrimination Causes

I t is time for society to begin to acknowledge the harm caused by discrimination against gay men and lesbians. It is time to own the damage done to gay people by heterosexist degradation, by isolating gay men and lesbians, by gay bashing, by the lack of laws that would protect and empower gay people, and by disowning gay and lesbian family members. It is time to realize that the suffering perpetrated on gay people reflects illness in the lives of the perpetrators. It is time to understand that this planet and all people on it are connected, and what affects one affects all.

If one person discriminates, then all people feel it. If one person hates, then the negative energy ripples penetrate everyone. If prejudicial people are not educated, then all people are guilty of accepting this disease and not stopping it. Gay men and lesbians have been in crisis for as long as the population has been oppressed. This fact has not been vocalized but must be in order to begin to understand the severity and urgency of the situation. Radical change is urgently needed to help the plight and advancement of lesbians and gay men everywhere.

If your house was on fire and you saw it but did nothing about it, there is a serious problem. You did not have the appropriate response to the situation. You should have reached out for help, dialed 911, and felt shock.

Allowing discrimination in society is the equivalent of all people seeing their houses on fire and doing nothing about it.

The heterosexist response to discrimination is inappropriate and confirms that people are missing honest gay education and healthy levels of empathy and civility. Instead, the majority of society is still being taught unhealthy and destructive heterosexist education from childhood through older adult years. Allowing this type of harmful education reflects the kind of illness that has been supported and promoted by homophobic people for centuries. Long-term discrimination, otherwise known as oppression, verifies that there is deep-seated, chronic illness in people everywhere. This kind of illness is not limited to only those who discriminate. Unfortunately, once a fire starts, the fire does not have the ability to confine itself to one area only. The same holds true of discrimination. When one person discriminates against a lesbian or a gay man, that discrimination spreads to, and is felt by, all people.

People everywhere need to be aware of this chronic disease that resulted from centuries of discriminating. This chronic disease eats away at the very fabric of civility and society. Oppressive fear, ignorance, and denial of the disease negatively affect families, the economy, spirituality, conscience, hearts and minds, communities, growth, education, and society as a whole. It holds everyone back from gaining true humanity.

The way that society will continue to develop healthier attitudes, beliefs, behaviors, and understanding toward gay people is by realizing that discrimination is taught, learned, unhealthy, and false; advocating for more gay people to come out and provide true gay and lesbian role models; stopping the transmittance of myths and unhealthy propaganda about gay men and lesbians; providing accurate and continuous education on real gay and lesbian history and lifestyles in schools and in religious organizations, at home, and in the media; increasing gay and lesbian strikes, protests, sit-ins, marches, and rallies; supporting gay and lesbian organizations and businesses; advocating for famous people to come out; denouncing gay and lesbian discrimination; advocating for the gay community; including gay men and lesbians in laws that protect heterosexuals; including gay men and lesbians in the laws ensuring heterosexual equality; arresting those who commit hate and violent crimes against gay men and lesbians and labeling the crimes as such; making gay marriage and divorce legal in all 50 states and on the state and federal levels; granting gay men and lesbians the right to be protected by the over 1,400 laws that are safeguarded through marriage; increasing gay and straight interactions and friendships to ensure real knowledge of, and experience with, the gay community; obliterating the "don't ask don't tell" policy and DOMA; changing and updating the language regarding gay men and lesbians to accurately and positively reflect the population; recognizing and rewarding the gay and lesbian population for its productivity and contributions to society; increasing the education of parents, teachers, hospital staff, police, the armed forces, lawyers, business owners, public servants, religious leaders, and the media on the gay and lesbian population in order to increase human rights, respect, and safety for the gay community and for all; helping religious groups that discriminate against gay men and lesbians realize their bigotry in order to stop it and, instead, evolve in the direction of love; genuinely feeling remorse over discriminating against gay men and lesbians and growing to respect and honor the population for its value and worth; and investing monetarily in gay causes and advocacy.

Gay men and lesbians urgently need to have somewhere to turn where there is truth, advocacy, respect, comfort, nurturance, empathy, and love toward the microculture. Everyone needs to have a safe haven where peace and growth abound. Gay men and lesbians also need these types of havens now more than ever to ensure the prevention of depression, drug and alcohol abuse, lowered self-esteem, suicide, danger, harm, homelessness, ostracism, and increased school dropout rates. Havens need not be built. Rather, the people occupying families, schools, churches, synagogues, the workplace, hospitals, human service agencies, TV, radio, the Internet, newspapers, magazines, and the community at large all need to welcome and embrace gay men and lesbians in word and in deed in order for the gay and lesbian community to feel that the earth is truly a humble, safe, and embracing haven and home.

All those who are discriminated against need to talk with each other more. Through talking and venting, people will get to know each other. They will become friends. They will learn each other's similarities and differences and that their similarities are far greater than their differences. They will help each other to not discriminate against each other and instead, love, trust, and respect each other. They will unite through their similarities and differences. They will begin to understand that they should not discriminate against others much in the same way that they do not want others to discriminate against them. They will begin to realize that those who know what it feels like to be discriminated against are guilty of an egregious act when they themselves discriminate against others.

People need to be taught that the most important life lesson is to love and respect others and themselves. This lesson is as important as being taught math, science, and history. This lesson needs to be taught to religious leaders and followers who discriminate against lesbians and gay men so that hypocrisy is banished and love and admiration are nurtured. Love and respect are given, received, and shared unconditionally and around the clock, not part-time. It is much harder to discriminate against someone once you allow yourself to get to know them. Learn about gay people and who they really are and are not. Learn how they differ from the myths that you have been falsely educated with. The more you get to really know those whom you discriminate against, the less you will discriminate against them, and the more you will begin to truly appreciate, respect, and like them.

CHAPTER 15

Gay Education 101

One Saturday afternoon in the summer of 2009, I walked into a major nationwide bookstore in Park Slope, Brooklyn, New York, and asked the help-desk worker to point me in the direction of the LGBTQ section of books. I was surprised when the man replied, "What's that?" I answered, "LGBTQ stands for lesbian, gay, bisexual, transgender, and questioning." He responded, "Oh!" and then guided me where to go. Later that day when I returned home, I called a university bookstore, asked the same question of the help-desk worker, and received the same answer. It was hard for me to fathom that this type of ignorance existed in one of the most liberal and most educated cities in the country.

It was then that I had the idea to call major university and major chain bookstores around the country and ask each help-desk worker, "Do you carry an LGBTQ section of books?" I placed 130 calls around the United States and at least one call to every state. The results were eye opening: (1) 86/130, or two-thirds of the help-desk workers in the bookstores did not know what the acronym LGBTQ stood for; and (2) 44/130, or one-third of the help-desk workers in the bookstores knew the meaning of the acronym.

The results of this simple survey revealed that the majority of people in the country are unfamiliar with the term "LGBTQ," which comes from gay education 101. These same uneducated people are responsible for voting on gay rights. I think that it is safe to say that if you do not know what LGBTQ stands for, then the odds are great that you have little education on gay people. One good thing that came out of making the 130 calls was that each person who did not know what LGBTQ meant was educated by me on what the letters stood for.

When I called the major bookstore chain in Baltimore, Maryland, a female help-desk worker answered the phone. I asked her if she had an LGBTQ section of books. She hesitated to answer. I then asked her if she knew what the letters stood for. She responded slowly and in a soft voice, "Does that have to do with gay and lesbian?" I happily responded, "Why yes!" She then let out a sigh of relief saying, "Oh good, I was afraid that if I were wrong I would have offended you." I gently explained to the woman that she had been offensive by assuming that I was heterosexual and would be offended by the words if I were; in her prejudicial or lack of gay education mentality; and in not thinking at all of the possibility that her prejudicial words were being addressed to a gay woman and the effect this would have.

At the very least, this experience pointed out to me that now, more than ever, increased outreach is needed to help people learn more about the gay community. Without continuous outreach, hopes for gay equality, support, and safety will remain only a dream. Gay people must devise and apply innovative ways to increase rights, which will expand and deepen gay consciousness. These efforts will help promote the gay movement and acceptance of the gay culture. One of the biggest enemies of advancement is stagnation. Stagnation is fortified by and results from fear, depression, lethargy, low self-esteem, and lack of education, whereas advancement evolves out of increased self-esteem, education, motivation, acts of advocacy, outreach, and invested monies in the cause. The gay community can accelerate advancement by maintaining good mental, emotional, behavioral, spiritual, and physical healthy living. Advancement must proceed throughout the world by employing a level of comprehensive education that will help eradicate discrimination and institute a future of gay and lesbian equality.

Chapter 16 relates true stories of prejudice and discrimination that gay men and lesbians face daily. The stories verify the need for increased education, advocacy, and protection for the gay and lesbian community. At present, there are not enough laws including the protection of gay men and lesbians. Otherwise, these stories of prejudice and discrimination would not exist to the degree that they do.

Without teaching law enforcement officers to enforce the laws equally and without bias, heterosexist and homophobic people will continue to commit crimes of hate and violence against gay men and lesbians and fail to realize the wrongness of the crimes.

Consequently, the incentive to repeat the crime will be reinforced, and statistics on crimes of violence and hate will increase. Gay men and lesbians will continue to suffer unnecessary invisibility, pain, harm, violence, and death at the hands of ill, discriminating people who were once innocent, loving children but taught by their parents to fear and discriminate against gay men and lesbians.

Increased education on gay men and lesbians needs to be provided to the police and armed forces for them to genuinely protect gay men and lesbians and to decrease their own discrimination against gay men and lesbians. Increased education needs to be provided to the clergy to eradicate their tradition of gay and lesbian demoralization and exclusion. Gay and lesbian education in the schools needs to increase in order to help prevent gay and lesbian depression, gay bashing, suicide, high dropout rates, and homelessness. Increased education needs to be given to people in the health-services field to ensure that gay men and lesbians receive the highest quality medical and mental health care and attention. In this way too, gay men and lesbians will not be discriminated against when wanting to donate blood or organs or when being treated for HIV/AIDS or any illness. Increased education needs to be provided in areas of housing and employment to ensure that gay men and lesbians receive equal treatment on the job and when purchasing or renting a home. Increased education needs to be provided in public arenas in order for gay men and lesbians to feel safe and secure in stores, in hotels, in business offices, on public transportation, and at social events.

The number of people needing increased education on the gay and lesbian community is high. There are not enough educators to go around. This fact reflects the level of progress made by the lesbian and gay community in helping people to decrease heterosexism and homophobia. However, much more work needs to be done in order for discrimination to subside on a grand level. If, for example, more judges would rule that lesbians and gay men should receive employee-based spousal benefits, then education in the legal circles would be deemed effective. Who will do the educating? The answer is simple: all those straight, bisexual, gay, lesbian, transgender, and questioning people who are truly educated to do so.

Providing real education on the gay and lesbian community is of the utmost importance because, without it, society will never fully understand that denying basic human rights to people because of sexual identity is an illness. For example, the U.S. House, Senate, Congress, and citizens voting on whether or not gay men and lesbians should have the legal right to marry should never have even been an issue because gay men and lesbians should be automatically entitled to the right. At this point in time, the gay community's eyes are opened wide enough to know that an ill society caused this issue to exist and that the time has come to demand their right to legally marry. Gay and lesbian lives should not be in the hands of politicians (uneducated on and discriminatory towards gay issues and lives) deciding their fate.

The gay community being denied the right to legally marry is criminal. The idea that this right of every other citizen is still up for debate is oppressive. It reflects the majority's lack of education on gay men and lesbians in the sense that the majority of society does not realize that this denial of rights is affecting real people. The majority of heterosexual society does not truly understand the pain involved when gay rights are denied because this pain does not pertain to the majority, or so they imagine. The majority of heterosexual society does not think about the emotional turmoil felt, for example, by the lesbians and gay men in California and Maine when they were granted the legal right to marry the person of their choice, only to have that right suddenly stripped away again.

People who never experience or see discrimination up close continue living in their own cocoon, prevented from gaining true understanding of the suffering of the victims; the opportunity to experience empathy for those discriminated against; and the education needed to realize the devastating effects of discrimination and the ways to decrease and end it. However, more people today do know and understand the plight of gay people. More people today do understand that the denial of rights to gay men and lesbians should be considered illegal and is ludicrous.

A group of African Americans are putting a bill before the U.S. Senate seeking reparations for their ancestor slaves who were discriminated against 160 years ago. Imagine the reparations due today to lesbians and gay men currently experiencing the pain and suffering in much the same way. Reparations should also be paid out to today's gay men and lesbians for the pain and suffering experienced by their ancestors.

The 1996 DOMA, passed by Congress and signed into law by Bill Clinton, represents the abuse of law to further promote and maintain homophobia and discrimination against gay people. This act, from a gay perspective, would have been more accurately titled the 1996 Heterosexist Obstruction of Gay Marriage Act (HOGMA) or the 1996 Defense of Heterosexist Marriage Act (DOHMA). DOHMA could have only been passed into law because oppression is, and has been prevalent throughout society for many years. Without heterosexism existing in society, DOHMA would have had no chance of passing. HOGMA represents the dire need for accurate and increased education about the gay community to prevent more heterosexist laws from being passed. DOHMA proves society's fear of gays, which hinders gay acceptance, protection, and support.

Connecticut, Massachusetts, Vermont, Iowa, New Hampshire, Washington, DC, and New York addressed the gravity of the problem of heterosexism when they legitimized gay marriage and, in doing so, provided respect and advocacy for the community. Gay men and lesbians who can move to one of these six states, or Washington, DC, should do so as soon as possible to acknowledge and reap the benefit that the enactment of this law provides; gain increased equality and protection in their lives; reward these gay-accepting areas of people for their empathy, support, and respect for all; reward the six states and Washington, DC, with gay presence and productivity; verify that legalizing gay marriage is healthy, civil, and lucrative for the state; provide the gay and lesbian community with increased unity; provide increased gay and lesbian presence in order for the majority to be exposed to, and to begin travel on, the path from prejudice to pride; and send a message to the rest of the country that gay men and lesbians will no longer subject themselves to the depravity of heterosexism and homophobia by living in the majority of the states that continue to deny them their legal rights and deny the country as a whole the real experience of unity.

The entire population consisting of heterosexist and pro-LGBTQ people will benefit from gay men and lesbians gaining rights, equality, and support. This fact needs to be understood in a real way in order for change to occur. Without gay and lesbian protection, the entire population is not safe. Without gay and lesbian advocacy, the entire population's civility is at risk. If people do not understand the immediate urgency of legitimizing gay men's and lesbians' rights, then it is impossible to continue living without admitting that illness and disorder rest in the very core of all people's hearts, minds, and souls. Pro-gay people cannot make this change alone.

Gay and lesbian advancement that has occurred until present time has been aided by those people, straight and gay alike, who have supported and helped facilitate gay and lesbian equality. Continued gains in the gay and lesbian community will only be successful if the number of people advocating for the community increases. This increase in the number of people who are pro-gay and pro-lesbian must also consist of straight people. Otherwise, advancement will continue to only be a dream, or nightmare depending on your perspective.

The end of the holocaust could not have come about through the work of Jewish people alone. Non-Jewish people needed to affirm the atrocity and support Jewish people to stop the holocaust. The same holds true of black slavery. Society needed to admit the cruel injustices perpetrated on black people in order to stop slavery and murder. The entire population suffered due to the horrors of the holocaust and slavery. The entire population gained increased civility, consciousness, and conscience by stopping these two atrocities.

There can be no advancement in the love of all people as long as some people are being discriminated against. Love and civility are the two seeds that must be planted, nurtured, and reaped in order for people to continue to exist and thrive. As long as oppression persists, which causes the seeds of love and civility to deteriorate, all of society will continue to exhibit mental, emotional, spiritual, and behavioral decay. If more people realize this fact, then the crossroads for positive change will be upon us, and a new day with a rainbow-filled sky will dawn.

CHAPTER 16

Personal Stories of Gay Discrimination

When heterosexist people bash, ridicule, humiliate, demoralize, segregate, ostracize, and murder gay men and lesbians, their words and acts are often unrecognized and unpunished. When gay men and lesbians press for rights in legal ways, heterosexist society often responds by claiming that it is under attack. This truth is both an irony and travesty. A prime example can be found in homophobic people's fear that they will turn gay if gay people possess equal rights. A second example was the Mormon congregation who proclaimed it felt attacked by gay people, when in reality they were expressing displeasure toward the Mormon leaders who helped pass Proposition 8.

This chapter contains personal stories of discrimination and prejudice experienced by gay men and lesbians on a daily basis. Prior to the interviews, the interviewer (the author) explained to the interviewees its purpose. Each interviewee willingly participated. These stories were related by gay men and lesbians and documented to verify that crimes of hate and violence against gay men and lesbians do indeed exist and go unpunished; to be used to help heterosexist people and all people understand the urgent need and reasons why gay men and lesbians must be included in the laws that protect, support, and deem all people equal and entitled to human rights; with the intention of helping to stop the stigmatization and mental, emotional, behavioral, and sexual abuse and oppression that occur in the community every day; and (4) with the understanding that each interviewee's identity would remain confidential and anonymous if requested.

INTERVIEW # 1

Ann Marie Petrocelli (the author), Interviewee #1: I am a 56-year-old white lesbian. I certainly am willing to discuss my life as a lesbian and views on heterosexism and homophobia. Being female and lesbian automatically started off my life with two strikes against me. Living in a man's world, I looked forward to less salary, fewer rights, less acceptance, less status, and less safety. Whose self-esteem and spirit wouldn't be dampened by not being born male, which comes with immediate and automatic gender privilege and entitlement attached to it? Born in 1955, I knew that I was attracted to women by the age of six. I kept this information secret because family, friends, the media, religious leaders, teachers, and peers made it evident in their derogatory words and actions toward lesbians that being lesbian was a bad thing. I also saw that all of the couples in sight consisted of only men and women, thereby making impossible the acquisition of real gay education from lesbian role models.

Families were composed of dad, mom, and children. Fathers went to work and earned the salary. Mothers stayed at home and took care of the kids and dad by cooking, cleaning, ironing, and shopping. I watched my mother and father and other moms and dads project their gender and heterosexual parenting roles daily. I also witnessed no same-gender partners among American families, which sent the mythical nonverbal message to all of society that gay life did not exist and that discussing the topic of gays was considered taboo and not to be tolerated. Heterosexist and homophobic messages of prejudice and discrimination against gays were delivered daily, sometimes in subtle and sometimes in blatant ways.

Realizing my lesbianism as a child helped me understand later in life that lesbianism is inborn. Innate lesbianism coupled with being born and raised female resulted in automatic diminished economic and social power and increased servitude to men. This realization helped me understand that lesbianism is about more than just sex between two women. It is as much about striving for economic, legal, religious, educational, political, and social balance and equality between men and women as it is about sex between two women.

I grew up trapped in an American nightmare where parents, siblings, relatives, friends, religious leaders and followers, teachers, classmates, media, and even other marginal groups verbally abused and actively discriminated against lesbians. I was handed this type of history on a tarnished silver platter from before birth. Odds were great that depression and low self-esteem would be in my future.

Now for me, at 56 years old, the American nightmare persists with the United States requiring lesbians to pay taxes while not being entitled to reap the benefits that the taxes pay for. Most straight people think that the gay community wants the legal right to marry for amorous reasons only. What most heterosexuals do not know is that marriage grants more than 1,400 rights to heterosexuals that gay folks are denied. As a lesbian, my paid taxes support those who discriminate against gays. I am caught on a double-edged sword of not being able to legally work without paying taxes while my paid taxes support the heterosexist majority's receiving the very rights that I am denied. The abhorrent denial of gay human rights influences lesbians to continue pursuing the goal of economic equality between men and women and changing the political, legal, and religious laws that discriminate against gays.

Religious organizations and their members must remember that the institution of marriage existed prior to the existence of religious organizations. There is no legitimate reason why religious organizations should be allowed to dictate who can and cannot marry. This dictation merely reflects anti-loving beliefs and behavior, inequality for all, allowed illegal acts, and the continued interference of church in state affairs. There is no legitimate reason why marriage, according to certain religious teachings, should be only for those couples who can procreate. This then means that if you are heterosexual and beyond child-rearing age, you should not be able to marry. It means that if you are infertile, then you cannot marry. If you are handicapped and not able to bear children then you cannot marry. What right do certain religious organizations have in deciding who can and cannot legally marry? More importantly, why is this illegal discrimination allowed?

There has been and can be no advancement in the balance of power and rights among all people without changing the laws to reflect gay and lesbian inclusion and safety. Imagine all out and closeted gay folks striking one day each year. Every home and workplace; every school and church; and every gay, straight, transgender, bisexual, lesbian, and intersex person would sit up and take notice of the value invested by gays that would be absent from society on this designated strike day. Imagine if all gay folks moved to Canada to gain the respect and equality offered by this country and to avoid USA oppression. What would the USA look, feel, and act like without the presence of gays? How would America be looked upon?

Americans are raised in a heterosexist, homophobic society regardless of living in a red or blue state. I grew up in liberal NYC and witnessed and personally experienced more discrimination than I care to remember. But I do remember. There are more gay people flocking to NYC imagining freedom and respect when they get here and gaining disappointment solely because oppressive people, laws, and institutions flourish here too. Still, the majority of the northeast is democratic and a haven for gays to flock to since discrimination is less in these states than in states that are predominantly red. Once New York state passed the same-sex marriage law, gay people no longer needed to (1) rethink the liberalness of the state and (2) move to those states that passed the law before New York did.

If the majority of people believed that the majority of society and the gay population were equal, then the entire economic structure would not be as it is currently structured. Political, legal, and religious laws help influence whether or not the economic structure maintains balance. Changing laws to reflect gay respect, rights, and protection have been and will continue to be a step in the direction of increased freedom, civility, equality, growth, balance, and inspiration not only for gays but for everyone.

If more people of marginal groups that are discriminated against supported rather than discriminated against each other, then discrimination would definitely decrease. More specifically, if more gays and lesbians stopped discriminating against transfolk, if more black, Asian, and Hispanic people stopped discriminating against gays, if more women stopped discriminating against women, if more born-again Christians and Mormons stopped discriminating against Jews, if more Jewish people stopped discriminating against black people, if more men stopped discriminating against women, then discrimination as a whole would lessen. Where would we be if all people shared an economic balance of power? Where would we be if the ultraconservative religious right wing were pro- and not antigay? Where would we be if marriage were the right of everyone? Where would we be if all people realized the consequences of preventing equality for all and of advocating equality for all? Where would we be if we all could experientially answer these questions because equality existed and was practiced by all?

It was very difficult for me to vote in 2008 when the majority of the presidential candidates opposed marriage for gays. I voted for Obama because I supported the majority of his beliefs. I did not support, however, President Obama's not supporting gays' right to marry, especially when he understood discrimination firsthand being a black man raised in white America. I opposed him and the USA on this level for allowing the continued oppression of the gay community.

Denying gays and lesbians the right to marry is a type of oppression that affords gay American citizens less equality than those not born in this country. How can anyone like President Obama, who originates from a group that is discriminated against, not realize the ignorance of inflicting discrimination on another when he has known and experienced that inequality? How is it that this brilliant man does not acknowledge that inequality experienced by one group means inequality for all groups? How do you support discrimination against another when you yourself have been the victim of discrimination and know that it is unjust and criminal?

To those blacks, Catholics, Muslims, Christians, Jews, Hispanics, Asians, Mexicans, and all others from minorities that discriminate against gays, I say, Wake up! Do you not yet realize that the very hate you experience as a result of discrimination you are inflicting on gays? Do you not yet understand life's vicious cycle in that the more you continue to discriminate against others, the more your group will continue to be discriminated against as well?

It is hard for me to believe that the majority of people are no longer prejudiced against black people. First, many black people state that they are still discriminated against after obtaining equal rights. Second, while black people gained equal rights reflected in written law, they obviously did not automatically gain equal rights behaviorally in everyday life experience. This reality exhibits the fact that actions, beliefs, and attitudes do not automatically change when the laws change. It takes many years of the laws reflecting equality to be in effect before people catch up to the laws and enact them cognitively, emotionally, and behaviorally.

Today, people still discriminate against black people even though the level of discrimination has decreased compared to, let's say, 60 years ago. If people really were not discriminatory against black people today, then I would venture to say that discrimination against gays would be less today too. If people today were truly reeducated and not discriminatory against black folks then they would have already realized the lessons and acknowledged in their words and behaviors that the prejudice and discrimination they were raised with about black people were all myths. They would then take this realization and reeducation, make parallels with gay prejudice and discrimination, and subsequently stop discriminating against this population as well.

I think too, that part of the reason some black people discriminate against gay people is because some black people never stopped believing the prejudices they were raised with about themselves. Consequently, they continue to be discriminatory toward themselves and their own marginal group. In other words, it is much easier to discriminate against another when you are discriminatory toward yourself. A second reason why black people continue to discriminate against gays is a religious one. More specifically, a percentage of black individuals belong to and abide by religions that discriminate against gays. There is the lack of understanding that discrimination toward one is discrimination towards all. Conversely, the more people are educated to truly dispel prejudices, the less they will discriminate, and the more they will love and respect themselves and others.

America needs to wake up to the fact that it is asleep regarding gay people and justice. When you educate heterosexuals on the real reason gays want the right to marry, most straight folks are, for the first time, enlightened to the fact of how many rights they gain through marriage that are denied to the gay community. Why should straight folks know anything about this denial of rights when the denial does not pertain to them or their lives? This is just another example of the majority of heterosexuals being raised in a heterosexist and homophobic society, unfamiliar with the gay population and plight, and blindly believing and supporting gay discrimination and hurt without question. This is just another reminder that increased levels of empathy will result only when the majority knows specifically what gay people are denied as American citizens from birth and how much gays needlessly suffer as a result of that denial.

INTERVIEW # 2

Interviewer (Author): What does the acronym LGBTQ stand for?

Interviewee #2: (Howard is a white, Orthodox Jewish partly closeted, partly out gay male social worker in his forties): Lesbian, gay, bisexual, transgender, and questioning individuals.

Interviewer: Would you feel free to relate your sexual orientation?

Howard: Yes. I'm gay.

Interviewer: Are you in, or out of the closet, or somewhere in between on the spectrum of gay identity?

Howard: I am somewhere in between.

Interviewer: How has the part of your life that is closeted affected your life?

Howard: I am not out at all in my Orthodox Jewish religious community. The fact that I'm not married and without children is a very separating, almost isolating experience. I have to be very careful about what is said or how I present myself to other people in the religious community. I am concerned about being asked to leave the community if my gay identity became known.

Interviewer: What is your attitude toward the Orthodox Jewish community?

Howard: It's a constant struggle within myself, between my family and me, and between me and other people in my synagogue because I have a lot of faith and respect for the religion. I know many people that have left the religion or became less observant as a result of coming out as gay or lesbian. I made the conscious decision to stay within observant religious Jewish life. I've done research on different interpretations on exactly what the different prohibition statements mean. I don't believe anything in the Bible is just at surface level. There are so many ways to interpret. There is so much analysis that is done on every word, on every letter. So definitely for the two or three sentences that are used in Leviticus against homosexuality, I believe that there are other ways to interpret them.

Interviewer: You chose to stay with the religion.

Howard: I feel that while I cannot deny being gay, I cannot deny being Jewish. I think I have it a lot easier now. When I came out to myself about 10 to 15 years ago, there were support groups that I used to attend for observant gay Jews. Now there is a very active, very high level of participation of gay observant Jews in groups at the LGBT Center in Manhattan and in a couple of synagogues in Manhattan and other places in the Metropolitan area. So, it's less lonely now because I know that there are other people out there going through the struggle and finding ways to deal with it. All different decisions have been made by people. Some have gotten married and had children. God bless them that they were able to do that.

Interviewer: How has being gay affected relations with your family and workplace?

Howard: My relationship with my family is so mixed. When I first came out to my family, I was labeled as mentally ill. I was referred to as a Nazi and finishing what Hitler didn't finish since I wasn't, or most likely wasn't going to continue the family name and lineage. I'm the only son in my family. A lot of hurtful things were said on both sides, by myself and by my immediate family. My parents have made such strides, God bless them, I don't know how. We have a very close relationship. They included my, unfortunately, now ex-partner in family functions, with the exception of anything that might involve my sister and her husband. My sister and her husband had nothing to do with me for a very long time. I was not allowed to see my nephews and nieces. If my ex-partner and I happened to be somewhere with my nephews and nieces, I was never allowed to hold them. Now, as long as I am by myself, my sister and her family now include me in family events. Each of them, at their own level of comfort, includes me in family affairs.

I think my parents' love for me helped them to include me in their lives. My heart aches for them since all their friends' children are married and have children. I can only imagine the turmoil my parents go through every day when they are asked why their son is not married because it is just so unusual in the Orthodox Jewish community for someone my age not to be married and not to have children.

Interviewer: How do you relate or respond to the prejudice and discrimination you experience from the Orthodox Jewish community?

Howard: In one way it's easy, because having gone to Yeshivah, I know what they learned. So in some ways, they feel like they have to be antigay because all we were taught in school is that homosexuality is evil and a sin. In Biblical times, gay people were stoned for acting out on their homosexuality. To expect someone who was brought up with these teachings and beliefs to immediately, or someday, be accepting, may just not be fair. I'm not saying that their discrimination is acceptable. At the same time, to expect them to change everything that they have been taught and led to believe is expecting a lot from them. I have to be very patient and hopeful that as they get to know me better and become more comfortable with me, they will be less antigay.

Interviewer: Are you at all homophobic or discriminatory toward yourself and the LGBTQ population?

Howard: This is one of my biggest struggles to not hate myself for being gay, for being who I am, and for not hating God. I may be self-centered for saying this, but I do not understand why God did not explain to me why I would be born into a family and community as someone that is so opposite and in contrast to what is expected by the Orthodox Jewish community. It is very hard for me to make sense of it.

Interviewer: Do you think you are born gay?

Howard: My parents think that I'm being tested and that I am failing my test. I can't imagine why I would have gone through what I have gone through and am still going through. I hope that I don't hate myself this much that I would do this to myself by making this decision. But I can't deny my feelings and my thoughts. If I felt that there was even a drop of heterosexuality inside me, then I would pursue trying to lead a heterosexual lifestyle. By age eight or nine, I sensed that there was something different about me. I continued to feel this during my teen years. I didn't come out until I was in graduate school. It just scared me too much to come out sooner. I was not accepting of myself enough to share the information with anybody else. It's crazy when I think about it now, that I honestly used to think that I had to sacrifice myself. I feared that I would be put into a mental hospital or put out on the street and lose all my family and friends.

Interviewer: Would you care to comment on where the LGBTQ community stands in terms of advancement of rights, protection, and equality?

Howard: I wish that we were much further along. Since the legalization of gay marriage in Massachusetts, nothing bad has happened. Yet people all across the country and even in Massachusetts are screaming that this is wrong. I don't see what's wrong about it. There is just so much fear in people. I'm not exactly sure what the fear is. Is the fear that they might have to deal with a certain level of homosexuality within themselves? Having worked with gay and lesbian youth, I do see more educators, more guidance counselors, and more teachers understanding and accepting of the gay and lesbian community. I think the message is to try and convince the LGBTQ youth that there are adults that they could speak with, trust, and connect with for help.

Interviewer: How would you like to see the LGBTQ community advance? What gets in the way of advancement?

Howard: I try to be out but I am still scared in different situations. I always think that if everyone LGBTQ came out, then it could make a world of difference because people would see how many gay people they know and are in their lives. I think that having that connection, actually knowing someone LGBT or Q does make a difference. I think that my parents have softer views toward gays as a consequence of having a gay son. I was 21 years old when I came out to my parents. As a home-care social worker, I am always afraid of my gay identity coming up with patients and their families. How will I deal with questions asked by them pertaining to my sexual identity? It's a struggle just doing the job because I am there for the patient. When you first meet the patient and are trying to develop rapport and trust and increased comfort with them, sometimes you do have to share some personal information. I think you lose a connection whether you are straight or gay when someone asks you if you are married and you are not, or if you have children and you don't. Any opportunity to educate is wonderful. I am sure that there are opportunities that I have let go. I also think that there are opportunities that I grasped. I remember at grad school at a conservative Jewish seminary, I stood up and spoke to a few hundred people. I came out to them because I felt at the seminary that there was a level of gay discrimination that I had to do something about. I had to speak out against it. I figured that I would deal with any repercussions that would happen. That is on a grander scheme. Whether I speak to one person or hundreds of people, or any group of people, I always have to be conscious of the words I am using. I have to know my audience and ways to reach them. I have to know how I am best going to challenge them to think about the issues and get them to see my viewpoint while I see theirs.

Interviewer: Outside of your family have you ever been discriminated against for being gay?

Howard: I have been called names and have lost friends when I came out. Even now I suspect people in my religious community imagine that I am gay after I have lived with a man for 10 years. These same people do not want to associate with us. Since I have never done anything to hurt them, I suspect that they do not want to associate with us because of our gay identity. A number of years ago, a film came out about Orthodox gay Jews. A lot of Orthodox synagogues sponsored viewings of it, which was remarkable. They were willing to address and face the issue. My only guess on why they did that was because more and more families today are being approached by siblings, children, and parents who are gay.

It's easier or less dangerous for religious people to come out today than it was 30 or 40 years ago. It is, however, still very difficult today to come out as well. I see families and the workplace being confronted with the topic more and more today. It is hard to work with someone if you don't respect the person because of their sexual identity. As one gets to know their coworker more, that leads them to question their homophobic beliefs more. Hopefully, getting to know gay people softens the homophobic stance.

Interviewer: What do you think of people who believe they are religious and simultaneously condemn homosexuality?

Howard: I don't think that it's the religions that condemn homosexuality. I think that it's the people interpreting the Bible that are discriminating against homosexuality. My father took a 13-week course on the first word in the Bible, *bereshiyt,* meaning "in the beginning." The rabbi went over all different interpretations of the first word in the Bible for 13 weeks. The rabbi went over every dot, every letter, how the word is connected to the last letter of the Bible of the written Torah.

In Leviticus it says that a man should not lie with another man. It is an abomination. To have no interpretation of what that means and to just condemn homosexuality and say that it is evil without understanding or analyzing what this could mean and just take it as a blanket, literal statement. The whole idea of keeping Kosher also comes from literal translation. For example, it is said in the Bible that you should not cook a young goat in his mother's milk. Where the heck from that do you get that you can't have meat and dairy together? Everything that we have to do with being Kosher started with this one phrase. If you want to take the Bible so literally then just don't cook a young goat in his mother's milk. And you wouldn't have everything else that follows about keeping Kosher.

I believe the Bible is from God. I also believe that we just don't have the capacity to understand everything that God is trying to tell us. To interpret the Bible in a hateful way just doesn't make sense to me. There are other ways to interpret or understand the Leviticus statements interpreted as against homosexuality. Some people say that it is only anal sex that is forbidden. For this reason, there are many religious gay Jews that will not engage in anal sex.

It does not make sense to me that God would create people in a manner that He finds detestable. I can't believe in a God that would be cruel like that. That can't be my God. I struggle with it. I'm not completely comfortable with who I am. In order for me to have some peace within myself, I've had to make it possible for me to believe that the prohibition is not the way that it is being interpreted by religious authorities because I love God. I hope and pray that God loves me and that He would not subject me and my family to the hell that we've gone through, and still go through.

There are not always people that I can talk to about my being gay and my gay struggles. My family, while accepting me, has not spoken with me about anything in regard to homosexuality in probably 10 years. It's like the pink elephant in the room. We know our son is gay and that the guy with him all the time is his ex-partner, but there is no recognition of anniversaries or the gay relationship other than including my ex-partner in only certain exclusive family events.

I don't want special treatment. I only want equal treatment. When I come out, it forces people to think differently. I did not have parents that were role models for gay people. As I was growing up, who was I supposed to talk with? I couldn't share anything with my friends or family. It just perpetuated the isolation, the loneliness, the feeling of exclusion, of being different and wrong in some way. When I first found out that there was a support group for observant gay Jews, it blew my mind. It was just by pure luck or fate or God's blessing that I was introduced to someone who sponsored such a group. I don't know that I would be alive today. If it wasn't for what I believe was God's intervention in introducing me to someone who was able to offer me support, at a time where I had nowhere to turn or no one to turn to, I might be part of the high gay suicide statistics.

There is excitement and yet anxiety, puzzlement, awe, and so many confusing and contrasting emotions when first meeting other gay people. All of a sudden I no longer felt alone yet still felt alone. It is a process. The first time that I was with people that I could really talk about me freely was liberating. Then, I had to repeat the situation in order to change the environment through educating others and through challenging myself to speak up, take risks, and hope and trust in God that all will work out.

INTERVIEW # 3

Interviewer (Author): Would you feel comfortable telling me one or several personal stories of discrimination that you have experienced? The stories will be included in my book in order to help confirm that discrimination against gays continues to exist and the need for laws to protect the gay and lesbian community as they do the heterosexual majority.

Interviewee #3 (Gregory is a 62-year-old black gay man): Yes, I am comfortable talking about ways that I have been discriminated against. I remember that there was an area in Central Park known for gay activities. They have this thing called the gazebo, where people go to relax, read, do whatever they want. I sat down for a few minutes at the gazebo. This was a time when, maybe, I was 26. I'm not exactly sure. This young man, maybe 20 or so, came over to me and started a conversation. We started talking. After a while, he said that he had to go. I told him that it was nice talking to him. Then, maybe 15 minutes later, he reappeared with about four or five different guys. I felt uncomfortable with them all looking at me and laughing, and yelling gay slurs. I got up and was about to walk away. Before I knew it, they all jumped me and beat me to a pulp. They worked me over real good. One of my friends had cautioned me about activities in the park. He told me to look out and be careful. I tried to be careful. This happened about 2:00 P.M. in the afternoon. Then, somebody approached while they were beating me up and yelled at them to leave me alone. So they all scattered. But by that time, the damage had already been done.

Another story of discrimination occurred when I was 17 years old. I met this group of friends. One of my friends had a contraption that you could catch birds that fell out of trees and then feed them. He asked me to hold it for him. Then he and my other friends were going to go to 42nd Street in NYC to donate blood. At that time, people were paid $5 to donate blood and it was not illegal for gays to donate blood. I went with my friends to the blood bank but waited outside for them because I was underage and could not donate blood. While I stood outside waiting for them to come out, it started pouring rain. People began waiting in doorways and under awnings. A police officer approached me and asked me, "What are you doing here?" I told him that I was waiting for some friends. I told him that my friends were donating blood. When they finished and came out, then I would go. He told me to move on. I told him that I wasn't doing anything. He walked away.

I remained outside the blood bank hoping my friends would come out in the next three minutes. Then, the police officer came back and said "You still here?" I told him that I didn't have any money to get on the train. So, I was just waiting for my friends to come back. He told me, "Come with me. I'll give you a token and put you on the train." So we went down to the train. We didn't go through the turnstile. We went through this doorway to this room. He told me to go into the room. We went in there and he closed the door behind me, took out his club, and proceeded to beat me in every way possible. The only part of my body that he did not touch was my face. He worked me over. Then he said, "Get out of here you fag and go home." So I made my way back to my friends who helped me.

My mother gave me just as much grief. She was always screaming and hollering at me. She had a boyfriend who always tried to toughen me up. He would tell me to go with girls. I used to "yes" him to death. I had a very good relationship with a boyfriend at that time. He was of age to have an apartment. He was an actor and was white. My mother was upset with me because he was white and because I was gay. I would see my boyfriend on weekends and would be out of my mother's house from eight o'clock in the morning to eight o'clock at night.

One night, at my mother's place, I was awakened by my mother and her boyfriend in the middle of the night. They told me that they had put my boyfriend in jail. When I was young, I was very emotional. I was terrified of what they told me. I got up and dressed. I went into the bathroom into the medicine cabinet and took what I thought was peroxide. I drank it all down. I was mistaken. It was not peroxide. But I thought at the time that I was doing myself in. They didn't go to the precinct. I went to my boyfriend's apartment and found him there. Later, my mother told me that I was lucky and that she just wanted this to stop. They tried to put a scare into me. My mother's boyfriend abused me a little bit. He smacked me and yelled, "Be a man!" I said, "I am a man." I told him, "I got everything that you got. It's just that I choose to use it with who I want."

I was timid and what you would call a little sissy when I was young. I was afraid of my shadow and a pushover. I was harassed in grammar school. I went to an all-boys' school. I got constant harassment. Every day I was in a fight. Girls would always laugh at me too. They thought that it was funny to always be grabbing at my clothes. One time, my schoolmates did push me too far and I went after them. I picked up a piece of glass. They ran faster than I could catch them. A police officer caught me and pulled me into the precinct and called my grandmother. My grandmother came and got me. It wasn't until my 30s that I started standing up for myself. I couldn't take anymore.

INTERVIEW # 4

Interviewer (Author): This interview is to be used in my book, *Prejudice to Pride.* I am obtaining personal stories of discrimination in order to help prove that (1) discrimination against gays and lesbians continues to exist; and (2) the need for laws that include the protection of gays is imperative. I ask that you please help the cause by relating your stories. Confidentiality and anonymity are guaranteed.

Interviewee #4 (Tanya is a 25-year-old African American lesbian): I'll help the cause. I am out, but not flamboyantly out. If someone asks me, then I will tell them. I've come into altercations mainly with males. I dress aggressively. I present myself as a female. One day, I accidentally rear-ended the car of a New Jersey driver. When I got out of the car, I saw that there was nothing wrong with his car. He was yelling and screaming. I told him to calm down. He started to come at my sexuality by saying, "You think you're a boy." At the time, I had just cut my hair short. I had on baggy sweat pants and a large t-shirt. He yelled, "You think you're a man. You want to be a man." He grabbed my wrist. I pulled my hand away and pushed him, letting him know that he was not going to disrespect me. I pushed him back but did not want to fight and get arrested. His friend got in between us and apologized. The driver was still very irate because I was a female yelling back at him and because of the way I was dressed. He brought up an issue that had nothing to do with the situation. Had I been a tall muscular man, he probably never would have said anything or run over to the car irate like he did. When the police arrived, I told them what happened and that the man, who was twice my age, grabbed and bruised my wrist. The police said that there was nothing that they could do about it. When I asked them what would have happened if I hit him, then they told me that they would have arrested me for assault. This was unfair because I felt threatened and totally dismissed, being a woman, lesbian, and young.

Interviewer: Does your family know that you are gay?

Tanya: I'm out with my mom and my brothers. My brother and I got into a really bad altercation about a year ago. My brother had come over to the house and started calling me all types of names, like you dyke, bitch, and you lesbian. So I was just looking at him and then I said, "Yea, I am gay and I do like women. I told him this and felt I took the power back from him." He asked me why I have to say anything to anybody about being gay. That's when I told him, "If you ask, then I'm going to tell you. It's who I am."

I first came out to my mother July of 2008, soon after I first realized that I was gay. I was drinking alcohol at the time so the words would just flow. She laughed and said that she knew. She told me that she was waiting for me to say something. My father used to always hit my brother and say, "He's going to be a faggot." My mother would say, "If he's going to be a faggot, he better be a damn good faggot because I'm not going to raise a half-assed faggot." My mother would always say, "If that's what you are, then that's what you are. I'm not against it."

I was surprised when my brother came over to the house and attacked my sexuality. It doesn't change who I am or anything about me. I thought possibly, that it was a desperate attempt to hurt me because I only told my mom and never told him that I was gay. He also felt hurt when I was in high school and told my mom, but not him, that I had a boyfriend. He didn't talk to me for about three months. It's been a year since he called me those names and we still haven't talked. I couldn't believe that he would attack my sexuality and me as a person, and he did it in front of my girlfriend. My brother and I used to be really tight, but not anymore. My mother raised us to be very accepting of people. So I think that he was trying to hurt me at the time.

I know that when my nephews say derogatory things, I put them in their place. One of my nephews is 10 or 11 years old. Three months ago, he said something about his teacher being a faggot. I explained to him that calling your teacher a faggot is like someone calling you the "N" word. It's just as bad. You don't use that word. At that point I was actually in college writing a paper for an inclusive class. The paper was about making yourself invisible. At that point I guess I made myself invisible because I could have said to my nephew, "You know, when you call him a faggot, it degrades me as your aunt because I'm gay. That's a derogatory term used toward me." I felt that I didn't need to out myself to my nephew at that time because he was still a little kid. My nephew's a really smart kid. He got what I was saying. He apologized to me saying, "I know that was a bad word. I don't mean it that way. It just came out." He has not said that word, or any derogatory or prejudice word, since in my company.

INTERVIEW #5

Interviewer (Author): I asked that you relate personal stories of discrimination, heterosexism and homophobia, which you agreed to. Is this information correct?

Interviewee #5: Yes, this information is correct. My name is Terry. I'm a 51-year-old white lesbian. I have been out since my young twenties. Certainly, after coming out, I was looking for a place to live, and found a place. I was there about three weeks. I had one female roommate. We were not involved. She was just a roommate. About three weeks after I moved into the apartment, the landlord came to the apartment with a police escort and said that we had 24 hours to vacate the premises. We were not behind on our rent and had not been served any eviction notice. We asked the policeman why we were being evicted. The policeman said it was because of unsavory character. In other words, the landlord had found out that we were lesbian.

Under the state laws, we had no protection. The landlord didn't have to serve us a 30-day notice. He could evict us at any point in time without notice. That's what he was doing. We had 24 hours to scramble and get all of our stuff out of the place and find a new place to live. The police were there to escort the landlord. We had no recourse under the law whatsoever. We lost our deposit. We lost that month's rent. We had to come up with new rent for a new place to live. That was one experience of discrimination.

Interviewer: How did you feel experiencing that ordeal?

Interviewee #5: I felt very lowly, like I had some kind of untouchable disease. I felt like I was less than an animal because I had no rights, no protection, and I was being treated like that.

Interviewer: Did you feel violated?

Interviewee #5: Yes, I felt violated and that I had no protection anywhere. Even though I was a law-abiding, tax-paying citizen, I saw that anyone, at any time could take away my job, my home, my child, anything they want because I was a lesbian, and lesbians had no protection under the law.

Another time in the late 1980s, there was a woman's music festival that was held annually in upstate Michigan. We would go the day before the gates opened and camp basically in our cars on the dirt road outside of the festival grounds waiting to get in the next day so we would be first in line. This was something that many women did every year. Every year, there were people that would drive by and harass the women in the roads. The police had been notified. Because that festival brought huge amounts of money, hundreds of thousands of dollars to the community, the police were supposedly cooperative with us, and every now and then would drive down that road to make sure we were all okay. They didn't do it very often. Even when they did, the people who were harassing us would just wait until the police were gone, and then come back.

There were families in cars, in station wagons, I remember, that would drive by and little kids would hold pictures up to the windows showing aborted fetuses assuming that because we were lesbian that, that somehow had to do with abortion. I guess also because we were feminist, but not everyone there was feminist. Not everyone there was even lesbian. The only requirement to get into the festival was that you were female. To these people, lesbian meant feminist, and feminist meant antiabortion, or pro-choice. Young guys would drive by and holler obscenities at us, like lesbian, dyke, man hater, sexual obscenities like "I'll show you what a real man is like" or "I'll change your sexual identity."

One year, in the early 1990s, some of these young guys started racing up and down the gravel road outside of the festival entrance. When you raced up and down, dust and rocks would fly up. We all would get into our cars and wait until they were done driving back and forth and yelling. One time, we hadn't heard them coming. Some of the women were in the road talking. They couldn't get in their cars fast enough. The young men ran three women down. The cars doors were taken off. The police never arrested anyone for it. One of the women died. One of them was paralyzed. She lost the use of her legs. I don't remember what happened to the third woman. Again, nothing was done. After that, there were more police that patrolled more often. I think they had let the people in the town know that they would be arrested if there were any hassles because they were pressured due to the death of one of the women.

The harassment didn't stop, but it lessened. There was never violence again. On this land, the women that owned the land couldn't build stages and structures because over the winter when no one was there, some of the people from the town would come onto the festival land and destroy whatever was there. Every year the women had to build temporary structures and tear the structures back down again before they left. It was an increased cost. Many people from the town, however, were supportive because we brought many hundreds of thousands of dollars into the area. People would fly over the festival and drop religious pamphlets trying to save our souls because they considered us all heathens.

Another incident happened in the early 1980s when I lived in Kalamazoo, Michigan. There was a group of young Hispanic men that the police knew about that were attacking gay men in the area. This went on for several years. The Hispanic men would beat up the gay men as they left the local gay bar. The young men put the gay men in the hospital. Some of them were severely hurt. The police, even knowing who the criminals were, did nothing. These gay men kept getting beaten up and put in the hospital. It wasn't ever written in the paper. I knew about it because I knew some of the people that had been beaten. They related to me how many men over the years had been beaten.

One night, a female friend of mine, who is very butch and looked masculine, was leaving the bar. This group of Hispanic men, a gang, pulled up in the car and started calling her faggot. They thought she was a gay man. When she turned around to yell back at them, like leave me alone, they saw she was a woman and it frightened them for some reason. They were out of their car ready to beat *him* up. When they saw that *he* was a *she,* it frightened them for some reason, and they hopped back in their car. There were four of them and one of her. Instead, they drove the car up on the sidewalk and ran her over, which broke her neck. She healed okay and ended up being okay.

The tail end of that story is that about five years later I owned a home in Kalamazoo. They still hadn't caught this young Hispanic gang. I belonged to a local lesbian organization that organized events and communication in the community. I had many lesbian events at my home. It was known in the neighborhood as a lesbian home. One day I was coming home from work and I saw a motorcycle up on my driveway next to my side door entry into my house. I pulled in the driveway and asked the guy if I could help him and what he was doing there. He said that his motorcycle had broken down and he had pulled it off the road to work on it.

There were two things wrong with that story. One, there was no reason to pull his motorcycle way off the road into my driveway next to my door because there was a four-lane road where he could have parked it to work on it, and have been out of traffic. The other thing was that he was very flustered when he saw me and when I asked him those questions. He hopped on his bike and it started right up, and he took off. He did not act like it was ever broken and knew that it would start right up, and it did. And he left.

A couple of days later, I was in my bedroom talking to my partner at the time. We were in bed. For some reason, I got out of bed and continued our conversation and began pacing around the bedroom. As we talked, I went to the window and saw that same guy sitting on his motorcycle in front of our house smoking. I knew he was up to no good because this was the second time he was watching our house. It was about 11 P.M. I turned to my partner and told her to call the police. Before I could turn back to look back out the window, I heard a crash. A taxi driver had come down the street and hit the guy on the motorcycle. The motorcycle was thrown a block down the road. The man was lying in the road screaming. The taxi driver was screaming. "I'm sorry, I'm sorry! I didn't see you!"

I thought this was unusual because the guy was sitting under a street light and was very visible. The guy that was on the motorcycle now lying in the street was screaming, "I'm sorry God! I'm sorry!" It sounded to me like he was at fault. My immediate reaction was that he felt that he was being punished for what he had been about to do. I didn't realize until later that this man, after talking to the police, was the leader of the Hispanic gang that had been attacking many gay men through the years. After, he was put in the hospital. I wasn't sure what happened to him. I never checked up on him. I know that he was severely injured. After that incident, the attacks on the gay men in the area stopped. There were no longer any gang attacks.

When I lived in Georgia, close to the border of Alabama, I found out that one of the strongest churches in Alabama had passed a state law saying any kind of mail that the church considered obscene could not be delivered in the state of Alabama. What this church considered obscene was, of course, anything of a sexual nature, even lingerie or sexual magazines, or any professional literature that mentioned homosexuality or LGBTQ, and could not be delivered by the U.S. Postal System. Here's a case of the state telling the federal government that they could not deliver anything that had to do with lesbians, or gay men, or bisexuals, or transsexuals, or questioning folks in a positive and professional way.

It was my boss that told me about this. When he told me, I asked him how a church could decide what I can get in my mailbox. He said that the church knows more and better than any government and was for the protection of the people. I told him that his church was not for the protection of me because it was keeping my life tethered. It was keeping me from receiving material that I do not consider obscene. He told me that he didn't want his daughter opening the mailbox and finding some literature on lesbianism. I told him, "First, don't order it in the mail. Second, if you're worried about it, then don't let your daughter pick up the mail. Why should your church decide what I can and cannot receive in the federal post office, and a political issue that is of concern to me or anyone else?"

If you aren't treated like every other citizen in the country, then you walk around thinking, even though you know that you are as good and as spiritually whole as the next person, that nobody else thinks that. Anyone I meet at any point in time can kill or attack me because of my sexual identity. I don't have any protection, whether it's about being beaten up on the street, or keeping my job, or raising my child, or living my life with who I choose to live with. I don't think special laws have to be made for gay people, or people of color, or other religions, or whatever the differences are in people. I think that we should all be included in the laws that already exist.

Why do they have to write this law for this person and that law for that person? Why can't we all be protected under the law? That's it, just be protected and have the same rights and freedom. Why does it have to be special for this person and special for that person? The laws are already there and written in the Constitution. The laws were supposed to be there to protect all men. We all inferred that that should include all women. In reality, they haven't included women either. It shouldn't be all men. It should be all people, period! It doesn't matter who you marry, who you love, who you worship, who you do whatever with. You should just be included in the laws, and protected in the laws, and have the same freedoms.

Index